MW01700589

Leap Into Living–Moving from Fear to Freedom

Gary Reiss LCSW, Ph.D.

Certified Trainer in Process-Oriented Psychology

CHANGING WORLDS PUBLICATIONS

Eugene, Oregon

Cover illustration by Kate Pryka, Pryka Graphics
Cover and book design by Christine Beneda, Beneda Design

International Standard Book Number: 0-9724300-2-4
Library of Congress Catalog Card Number: 2004093141

First Edition 2004

Address all inquiries to:
Gary Reiss
412 W. 17th
Eugene, OR 97401

Email:greiss@igc.org
Website:http://www.garyreiss.com

Dedication

I am dedicating this book to my father, Barney Reiss, who taught me so much about living and dying.

Acknowledgement

First I would like to thank Dr. Arnold Mindell, the founder of Process oriented Psychology. He has been my main guide down the river of learning, helping me to move beyond fears of life and death. He has also been a great friend and support for my writing and in so many other aspects of my life. I also want to acknowledge Dr. Amy Mindell for her work and support in the area of working with coma patients. She, along with Dr. Arnold Mindell, has created Process oriented coma work, which provides a place where I have been able to learn and apply what I am learning. Many thanks to my parents for their continuing love and support of my writing, and for so strongly believing in me. Also, for being the kind of family where we can discuss issues like the ones this book raises, openly. Much appreciation to Sharon Emery for her help with the layout of the book, for our continuing discussions in this area, and her ongoing support. Thanks to BJ and my daughter Eliana, for being there with me, spending so many years together while I struggled so with these issues. Also, much appreciation to Leslie Heizer for the technical work, friendship, and support she offers in editing my books, and Sheya Rondeau for her editing. I also offer so much appreciation to all of the people I have worked with as clients over the years, who have all been my teachers in this area of living and dying. Finally, I am thankful to the Creator who granted me the privilege of being born, and being alive to write this book, and to participate in the process of becoming an eagle.

TABLE OF CONTENTS

INTRODUCTION

One day, when walking in the mountains, I was thinking that when people are really free to leap into living, they live and die with the freedom and grace of eagles. Then, when I reread Sogyal Rinpoche's *The Tibetan Book of Living and Dying*, I found a beautiful quote expressing the same idea. He refers to his spiritual teachers as mountain eagles, saying that they "soar above both life and death and see them for what they are, in all their mysterious, intricate interrelation. To see through the eyes of the mountain eagle, the view of realization is to look down on a landscape in which the boundaries that we imagined existed between life and death shade into each other and dissolve."[1] From the standpoint of the eagle, one neither fears, nor does not fear, death. What is just is. You live freely, and therefore, are free to follow your deepest inner callings, and follow your heart in daily living and in facing the moment of dying. To have this perspective allows you to leap into life. I hope that this book will help us all become freer, like the eagle. The question then becomes what do we do with this freedom, how do we live our own lives, and live for the benefit of others, from this place of full living? The other implication of this freedom then is that when our time of physical death does come, we will face this with a sense of equanimity. Those people who I have worked with who have reached this level of personal development live and die listening to the beat of a different drum.

I have always been an adventurous person who loves living life on the edge, whether it is skiing down a steep slope or working in Israel with century-old conflicts. Part of my love of life has always been with me. Another part, I am gaining only now, in middle age.

Despite my love of adventure, I have also gone through periods of intense anxiety about illness and dying. The two times I suffered most from these anxieties were in adolescence and during my mid-life years, particularly from the ages of thirty-nine to forty-three. About ten years ago, I felt called to get to the root of my fears concerning illness and death; I was also curious about why they happened during certain periods in my life. As I began studying anxieties in relation to health and death, I noticed similar patterns in many of my clients, i.e., that health anxiety tended to increase at times of rapid change in life.

For example, teenagers, not normally worried about health, found an outbreak of acne and decided they had cancer, while adults with no history of hypochondria were suddenly panicked about seemingly innocent health issues. Here is a typical example: At around age forty, a man decides to have medical tests performed because his arm is sore. The test results come back perfectly normal, but he is still quite worried about his general health. I might say, "Have you been doing anything lately that might make that arm sore?" He might respond, "Yes, lifting weights at the gym." At most times in his life, he would not be requesting medical tests over a sore muscle, but at mid-life, a time of increased change, his anxiety level has suddenly increased.

I began my research into anxiety concerning illness and dying by exploring my family history. In general, my family members tended to be very worried about their physical symptoms. My family also has a history of significant health problems and an increasing number of family members are medical doctors. As we will see, each of these facts influenced the development of anxieties. Next, I looked for collective issues that influenced my anxiety, including my being Jewish. I had noticed higher levels of body-related anxieties among my Jewish clients than in clients from other backgrounds. At first I thought this observation might come from some kind of internalized prejudice I carried towards my fellow Jews, but I found many other therapists who had noticed the same tendency. I will address this collective influence in the chapter on Jewish approaches to anxieties about the body.

Next, I began to look at Western culture, which emphasizes rationalism, technology, and science. I had noticed that people from non-Western cultures had a much less anxious attitude towards death than people in the United States and Europe. For example, I remember walking in the holy city of Vernassi, near the Ganges River in India. Many people sat or lay in the streets waiting to die. When a person died, the body was carried through the streets to be burned in the sacred fires on the shores of the Ganges. While death was present everywhere, anxiety was absent.

Western culture has influenced our collective attitudes towards our bodies, specifically death and illness. Growing up, I had thought that as I gained more knowledge of the body, I would feel more peaceful about my health, but knowledge did not necessarily relieve me. As an adult, I asked my brother, a cardiologist, if the doctors he knew seemed peaceful concerning illness and dying. He said that actually they were quite anxious about their health. This statement, along with my own experience, led me to explore approaches from other cultures in order to develop inner peace around my body anxieties.

I have been greatly aided by my exploration of spiritual traditions that offer other views of the body, including Zen, Tibetan Buddhism, Jewish Mysticism, Taoism, and Native American teachings. In addition, my personal work with the founder of Process-Oriented Psychology, Arnold Mindell, has helped me work through and move beyond my fears about illness and dying. The exercises and theory in this book owe much to my studies of Process Work.

I will never forget one encounter I had with Mindell. I told him I was afraid of dying because I was having various body experiences, none of which were related to a serious illness. Mindell said to me, with a twinkle in his eye, "You are very close to dead, and for your happiness, I can't wait until it happens." He made it clear that he wasn't talking about my physical death. Instead, he was referring to the part of my life that needed to die, and other parts pressing to live. I was so freaked out by the transition happening in my life that I was panicking over my health. With humor, Mindell guided me through the death of my personal history and attachment to my old identity with all of its hurts, limitations, and fears. Through this work, he helped me identify with my larger potential as a human being. For example, when I recently turned forty-seven, he told me to create a little ceremony at my birthday, in which I should bury the old part of me and talk about what was going to live from now on. It was not only a powerful ritual, but lots of fun. Once I finished, many people started to laugh and created funny names for me for the next part of life. After this brief "funeral," I suddenly felt much freer and younger!

I am not saying that illness and death are not scary. Some fear of dying and death is natural. The fear of death can help us wake up to the fact that life is limited, that we need to move forward and not live as if we have forever. Fears of death are like phone calls from the depths of our being that differ according to people's different life directions. For one person, it is some part of their personal histories that needs to die, and a new phase of life is coming. For others, it means that they have reached a momentary edge, a place in their personality, that they are stuck in and feel the need to get past. Yet others get anxious about death, as they have so much they still want to accomplish in this life. People become anxious about illness and death when they feel distant from that part of themselves that is coming through in their dreams, and trying to guide them. One other common theme is that people are anxious about death because they need to work on the kind of states of consciousness that surface around dying, long before the moment of death arrives. Death can serve as an ally that helps us learn to live our lives fully, as if today were our last day, so that when the last breath comes, we have learned to live fully every moment, and the moment of death becomes one more moment. We will explore the concept of death as an ally throughout the chapters that follow.

I intend this book especially for those of us who are sometimes gripped by panic on the subject of illness and dying. Panic is one of the most painful of human emotions, and for those who greatly fear illness and dying, death does not appear to be an ally. In fact, we are held back, at times even paralyzed, by our anxieties. As I move beyond this fear, I find increasing energy, clarity, purpose, excitement, and periods of deeply felt peace and well being. I am reminded of Fritz Perls, who used to say that the only difference between anxiety and excitement is remembering your breathing. I would even go a step further and say that the only difference between anxiety and excitement is working on oneself in order to move closer to one's own deepest Self. Through this new perspective, anxieties about death and illness become our friends, calling on us to follow our dreams, and live and die with awareness, and with the freedom of the eagle that soars above.

The journey beyond fear of illness and dying is physical, psychological, and spiritual. The Buddhists are especially adept at teaching that one learns how to live through meditation on one's death. I hope not only to help us face the inevitable fact that we will die, but also to help us have the courage to face our anxieties and our death, thus gaining the awareness and personal power to live life fully. If a person has enough awareness and detachment to relate to the eternal in each moment, that person becomes similar to a Zen master who lives life fully until their last breath. People who live with this awareness seem fully alive and fully dead at the same time. They are alive to themselves and their worlds; at the same time, they are dead to their personal history, old patterns that lock them in, attachments that keep them from being free.

The journey from living with fear to living freely requires moving from a rational, mechanistic view of life, the body, and death to a more holistic perspective. This new perspective includes the body as a place where dreaming and spirit are at work, where death is not just an end but also a beginning, where life and death are experienced not as polarities but as ongoing cycles. Living this way brings us to a centered peace from which we can face the polarities present in all aspects of our lives. I hope that the theory, stories, and exercises that follow help people move closer to their own sense of being mortal, to knowing that death is close and it is always a good time to live fully in the present. I also hope to convey the sense that we are all connected to something eternal and that all that comes to pass in the span of a lifetime is part of a larger plan. Being strongly connected to something eternal can be a path of tremendous relief, energy, and gives people the power to follow their dreams, and to leap into a life of creativity, passion, and meaning.

In the final section of the book, I explore through my own life, and through case histories drawn from my twenty-seven years as a therapist, people's stories of moving freely through life and death. Leaping into living means new approaches to work, body symptoms, relationships, world change, spiritual practice, sexuality, and all other major parts of our lives. By looking at other's stories, we can gain the inspiration and courage to move forward in our lives past the old patterns that hold us back. Living freely makes dying freely much more likely, we can let go as we have fulfilled the purpose of our journey here, and view death as the next adventure.

PART ONE

Eastern and Western Approaches to Life and Death

| CHAPTER 1 |

Western Views

Die while alive
And be thoroughly dead.
Then do what you will.
All is good. –Zen Master Bunan

Here in the West, death and life, illness and health, seem separate. Life and health are to be pursued, death and illness to be avoided. Life and health are associated with success and possibilities, while illness and health are associated with despair and defeat. If a person is ill, the implication is that something is wrong with them. In many families, death has replaced sex as the forbidden topic.

In my therapy practice, clients continually demonstrate the value in so-called illness. Part of my work is with people in comatose states. When I first started working with coma patients, I thought that no fate could be worse than lying in a hospital, hooked up to tubes, dependent on a medical system and machines to keep you alive. As I worked with people, every coma patient who came out of the coma enough to talk has said that the coma was an incredibly transformative experience. One young man, whom I met while he was in coma after an auto accident, later said that without the coma, he would still be in the same stuck place in his life. The many comatose people I have worked with woke me from my own sleep state, in which I saw illness only as mechanical failure that put people into the technologically efficient hell of being kept alive by machines.

Similarly, another man I worked with, until he died of cancer, told me that he was much more alive approaching death than he ever had been prior to this experience. He said that he had been ignorant of the meaning of life for many years before his illness. After the illness, he discovered a deep spiritual nature. He spent his last days loving his family, his friends, and his community. At a self-organized good-bye celebration for himself, he sat like a Buddha, greeting his community with utter radiance.

These stories are not meant to imply that both of these men did not suffer or feel afraid, frustrated, and depressed about their conditions. Yet, given the opportunity to work on their experiences, each found a deep meaning that transcended pain, suffering, illness, and in one case, death.

Positive Death Experiences

Here is another story that illustrates the potentially transformative nature of the dying experience. I worked for quite some time with a woman who was dying of kidney failure. She had worked through all the unfinished business in her life and made peace with her family, her church, herself, and her Creator. Finally, she made the decision to remove herself from dialysis, which she felt there was no point in continuing, now that she was at peace with her inevitable death. I was out of town as she was nearing death. One day, I called to see how she was doing. The person who answered the phone said that she had been in a coma and had not spoken a word for many days. I asked them to put the phone to her ear. "Hello Jane," I said, "its Gary. I called to see how you are." She answered and asked where I was. I told her that I was teaching in Salt Lake City. I asked, "How are you doing?" She said, "Wonderful!" She said that she was experiencing a peace the likes of which she had never known. She had even spoken with her pastor, with whom she had been furious, and made peace. I told her that she was an awesome woman who had done more relationship work in a short period of time than many people do in a lifetime. I told her I loved her and wished her a good journey. She told me how much she loved me and promised me she was going to have a great trip. When I got back to town and checked the nursing home records, I found that she had died within hours of this conversation.

These stories raise a number of large questions: What is time? If death is a horrible fate to be avoided at all cost, how can people die in bliss? What is the difference between quality and quantity in living? Many Taoist masters and Western doctors consider longevity an important goal in life, but what are the advantages of a long life? What is a coma? How could the woman in the story come out of a coma to have a conversation? How much choice do we have around the timing of when we die? Why do many doctors tend to make us feel so badly about being ill? Why don't more physicians talk about the exciting chance for awakening, growth, healing, and transformation present in our symptoms? What is the function of love in healing, in living, in assisting those dying?

In many ways, these questions are like the Zen koans, or questions, that people meditate on in Zen monasteries. With a koan, meditating on the question is more important than coming up with an answer, because meditating sets off an internal process. We will be investigating these questions from different angles throughout the rest of this book.

Death and Illness as Terrifying

I have heard many sad stories about people who die in fear, with no one to help or guide them. Those who face death with terror often do not believe in anything spiritual beyond this life. As one person told me, their dying loved one's view was that you died, were put in the ground, and rotted. Of course this person was terrified of death. When someone is dying afraid, families are often relieved that death ends not only the physical suffering, but also the hellish emotional states. When people in the West die today, it is usually in a hospital. Rarely do people die at home, with friends and family to guide them between states of consciousness, particularly the altered states that occur near death. Often people particularly fear dying alone in an impersonal hospital, with tubes all over the place – a techno-finish. This view of death dominates the minds of many of us in the West. We don't tend to picture death as a state of peace, ecstasy, union, or completion.

Many people associate illness with long stints in waiting rooms, short visits with their doctors, frightening tests and waits for test results, and drugs that sometimes make the person feel worse than the illness did. Recent news reports suggest that there are some real reasons to be scared when dealing with the modern medical world. With all of its wonderful, helpful aspects, there are also terrifying aspects, such as avoidable medical errors. The topic of medical errors is so hot that former President Clinton had addressed it several times, and Congress has been investigating how to help hospitals limit avoidable medical errors.[2] A recent study conducted by the American Medical Association said that in nine out of 10 situations where doctors had patients in for routine office visits, the doctor did not discuss issues enough to allow the patient to make an informed choice.[3] Thus, patients often feel, and rightfully so, that they have no control over major medical decisions. Finally, illness can seem even more frightening when one is faced with large medical bills, or clashes with insurance companies. These stresses may make people more ill than their original disease or medical problem. Chapter 9 explores problems with modern medicine and its relationship to fears of illness and dying in more detail.

Another factor that contributes to people's fear of illness is that many psychologists, alternative practitioners, and physicians somehow imply that people who get sick are personally responsible for their illnesses. The last time I gave a speech at a hospital, the person who invited me to talk said that if I described how patients who were ill were responsible for their illness, she would hate me, since this would not be helpful to them. I told her not to worry, because I consider illness a dreaming process. If we consider illness a dreaming process, there is no point in asking someone to take responsibility for it, just as it does not make sense to ask someone to be responsible for what they dream about at night. Once a person becomes aware of the whole process behind their illness, they can make choices and decide if they feel responsible for any element of the illness.

Symbolic Work With Symptoms

Arnold Mindell explains the role of dreaming and dreamlike symbolic experiences occurring in the physical body in his first book, *Dreambody*. Mindell uses the word dreambody to describe that part of us that is both the physical body and the dreaming patterns behind physical body experiences.

Here are some brief examples of the dreaming body. When working on a breast lump, a woman tells me that the lump is like a hard rocky mountain, immovable. She describes herself as someone who is not able to hold her ground and is always adapting to those around her. The lump is outside her identity, a dreamlike experience of firmness that she wants more of in her life. As she worked on incorporating this solid quality into her behavior, the lump actually disappeared.

From the dreambody perspective, eczema might be experienced as a great cat scratching herself. Dizziness might be like a whirling dervish reaching for God. One woman experienced a mass in her ovary as something too big for its container. While working psychologically on the mass, she began to leap for the sky, as if ordinary life was too small for her. After working with many people on their actual experiences of symptoms, I have come to believe that something meaningful, relevant, and symbolic always emerges from physical symptoms. This holds true regardless of whether the person is very experienced in terms of personal growth, or has little experience with personal growth work.

Symptoms sometimes disappear after such symbolic work. For example, I remember a young woman with chronic severe stomach pain. When I asked her what the pains were like, she said they were stabbing pains and made a motion with her hand. I gave her my pen and she played with it as if it were a knife, stabbing a pillow. Soon she had an image of stabbing her father, in fantasy, to get even for all the ways he had deeply hurt her. I played the role of her father while she was carrying out the stabbing, and had her tell him what she was feeling. She was supposed to have exploratory surgery the following week, and it was canceled because her pain disappeared following this session.

If our body's experiences are dreamlike, and if we are not able to relate to these dreamlike aspects, then illness and death become terrifying. We become like actors on a stage, thrown in front of the audience without knowing the story we are a part of. Life becomes terrifying. We have no control, and our bodies are often seen as our enemies. Symptoms are something to be defeated; we declare war on certain diseases without seeing what is really happening in the dreaming background of the symptom.

For example, I have worked with many people who suffered severe abuse in their past. In such cases, a medical practitioner, or therapist, might unconsciously start to act just like the worst part of the person's nightmare. For example, a person with neglectful and abusive parents ends up with a doctor who neglects and abuses them without understanding that the symptom, the doctor, and the patient are all part of an ongoing nightmare. If this happens unconsciously, everyone loses. The patient may be re-traumatized, the doctor may end up with a malpractice suit, and life becomes hell for all involved.

This story can also have a different ending. If doctors and patients become aware of the dreaming background of symptoms, the patient may be able to use the illness experience to transform the sense of being a powerless victim of life. The doctor may be able to learn more about communicating and working with an abuse survivor. In such a case, the symptom becomes a transformative agent. For example, I referred a patient to a doctor. During the visit, the doctor's attempt to relieve her anxiety by acting very knowledgeable as he defined and labeled her symptoms re-stimulated her abuse issues. She felt frightened and that his outer authority overrode her personal knowledge. I encouraged her to talk to the doctor about it. She did, and the doctor apologized and said that had had not meant the statement in that way. The doctor stated his comments about her illness in such a way that the patient felt comfortable and relieved; she was now eager to work on her symptoms with this doctor. In this case, the doctor gave the client a new experience. He accidentally violated her by not responding to her feedback, but then he supported her to speak up for herself. He also changed to follow her directions. Thus, the patient had an experience of being trusted and encouraged to trust herself. This experience itself was quite healing, even before any of the medical interventions began.

If those of us who are helping professionals do not view life as dreamlike, we may become like our patients' or clients' worst nightmares. Even if we can make a technical fix of their bodies or their behavior, we may perpetuate the same patterns that they have suffered from their entire lives.

Western Scientific Rationalism and the Body

In *Dreambody*, Mindell shows that we can benefit from having not only a materialistic but also a mystical view of the body. He draws on his background as a physicist to provide an overview of different theories of the body, then places these in a historical context of the development of science.

> Like medicine, modern physics has been dominated by Greek and Christian thinking until modern times... However, twentieth

> century research has forced physics to reject the Greek conception of geometrical time and space. Surprisingly enough, the new concepts of modern quantum mechanics are similar to Eastern views of matter… Physics, the most rational branch of modern science, has produced a sort of subtle body view of nature. Matter is both solid and formless energy.[4]
>
> If we adapt this development to the body, our next step is to build a view of the body that is both solid and formless, and to work with our fears so that we are not just afraid of the solid body, but have the fearlessness associated with connecting to the eternal body.

Mindell goes on to say,

The real body is the product of cultural concepts. Today, in the "civilized world," the body is composed of heart, lungs, RNA, bacteria, cells, and diseases. In contrast, the dreambody is created by individual experience, personal descriptions of signals, sensations, and fantasies, which do not necessarily conform to collective materialistic definitions. Both real body and dreambody descriptions are valid within their own observational realm.[5]

The implications of this are that mainstream views of the body are no longer relevant to the whole person. Mindell reaffirms what the woman above learned in the interaction with her doctor. When it comes to dealing with our dreaming experiences, our dreambody, trying to make collective, classical definitions is not enough. How a person experiences their body and their symptoms may be very different from a collective definition.

For example, I remember working with a woman who had been diagnosed with terminal cancer. As she worked on herself, she said that she felt better than she had in years, both emotionally and physically. As she became closer to herself, she stopped asking for her latest blood cancer counts and other details of her disease. She wasn't in denial about the seriousness of her disease, and talked at great length about the possibility that she might die in the near future. However, she was much more interested in her own reality of feeling increasingly well and whole than in focusing on the scientific data about the progression of her disease.

Mindell points out that matter, and therefore the body, was seen as solid and fixed until quantum physics came along. If matter is fixed, it makes sense that the body is mechanistic and that medicine will consist of materialistic diagnoses and solutions. From this perspective, there is no need for a physician to collaborate with a patient to reach an informed consent decision. From this perspective, medical decisions appear to be straightforward mechanical decisions. However, if we take the perspective of quantum physics into account, we need to consider the implications of subtler, dreamlike experiences, where time and space themselves are only relative concepts of limited use.

If we use the mechanistic scientific view that existed prior to quantum physics, the patient's experience doesn't matter, because the body is a machine that will react in one predictable way. When we move to the quantum physics perspective, we need a view of the body that studies and treats the symptom within the context of individual experience. Without this view, our experience as patients is terrifying. If we don't shift our view of the body away from the mechanistic perspective, we can't shift our approach to patients. In the mechanistic perspective, the patient's experience is irrelevant. For example, a woman went to the emergency room. She begged the emergency room doctor not to give her medication that she knew she was allergic to. Despite her specific request, he followed his own thinking and gave her a medication that he said would not bother her. She took the medicine and ended up back in the emergency room, as it almost killed her. If a patient's experience is not validated, such situations easily occur.

Considering the patient's experience may come down to a matter of life and death. For example, I was called as a consultant on the case of a patient in coma. The doctors had recommended removing life support. After working with the man for about six hours, I told the family that I thought he might recover, at least to some degree, and I did not think the situation was totally hopeless. I based my statement on the man's response to the coma work. He was particularly responsive with his movements, moving first one arm, then both arms, then his legs and hips. He also followed me with his eyes, which appeared to fill with tears in emotional response to some of the things I was saying. The family said that this was the most active the man had been since entering the coma. After five days of working with the man, he was up, beginning to speak, move, feed himself, and take steps. The doctor told me he still did not consider this significant change, according to his model, because the patient still was not speaking in complete sentences. The doctor's model and the patient's experience were far off. The doctor finally admitted to me that the patient was doing much better than five days ago, when he was on total life support. After a few more days, the man was speaking in complete sentences and paragraphs. If the patient's experience had not been considered and worked with, the patient, the family, and the doctor would all have been deprived of his recovery and continuing life experience.

Summary

Modern medicine has not yet moved in the direction suggested by quantum physics. The body is still viewed primarily as a machine. The individual is usually not considered of prime importance and solutions are prescribed for symptoms rather than for unique people. This view of treatment makes it difficult for people to connect with their own experiences. Robbed of a sense of meaning, illness and death do not help bring people closer to the spirit that breathes life into them. Instead, they are out-of-control experiences of apparently purposeless suffering. Each person's family system, cultural background, and individual psychology determine how terrifying these experiences are, and in general, illness and death are frightening for many people. In many cases, the experiences around treatment are far more difficult than the illness itself.

It is time for transformation to a model that includes both body and soul, both physical and spiritual medicine. If we adopt this new perspective, the body, illness, and death are no longer solely terrifying, but provide potential for meaningful transformation.

Feel free to skip any exercise if it makes you feel too uncomfortable.

EXERCISE: Find a place where you can sit and meditate for a while. Bring a pen and paper.

Pick one of the following questions and meditate on it. As you meditate, write down whatever insights you have, even if they seem irrational. Especially become aware of what pops into your mind spontaneously.

1. What is time?
2. If death is a horrible fate to be avoided at all costs, how can people die in bliss?
3. What is the difference between quality and quantity in living?
4. What are the advantages of a long life?
5. What is coma?
6. How could someone come out of a coma to have a conversation?
7. How much choice do we have around the timing of when we die?
8. Why do many doctors tend to make us feel so bad about being ill?
9. Why don't more physicians talk about the exciting chance for awakening, growth, healing, and transformation present in our symptoms?

You may wish to write down your thoughts in each of these areas. When you finish the book, write down your opinions again, and notice if or how they have evolved.

In the next several chapters, we will explore how major Western, Eastern, and Shamanistic methods deal with illness and dying in ways that can alleviate some of the anxiety and suffering common in these parts of life.

| CHAPTER 2 |

Jewish Views

Modern Jewish views and the History of Jewish Attitudes Towards Health

In the small, mostly reformed Jewish world I grew up in, people were extremely neurotic about health. My family and friends spent lots of time in doctors' offices, whether as doctors, patients, or both. Woody Allen brought a great deal of humor to this subject. I remember roaring with laughter when people talked about their symptoms in his movies, recognizing similar scenes from my childhood.

It is important to say that this observation stereotypes Jewish people. I have met Jews at every point on the spectrum around their health; from the most uptight to the most relaxed, from the most mainstream to the most alternative. Yet, I believe that if a survey were done, a higher percentage of Jews, as compared to people from other backgrounds, would exhibit anxiety about health, illness, and dying. This has been my experience with people from all branches of Judaism, including Reform, Conservative, Orthodox, Reconstructionist, and secular Jews. I have several theories about why anxiety around health and illness appears to be common amongst Jews.

In *Jewish Reflections on Death*, Jack Reimer sums up what has happened to modern Jews. He says, "The Premodern World knew a full measure of complexity and tragedy. There were forms, clearly defined and generally accepted forms, with which to celebrate life and with which to commemorate death. And there was a faith, a many-sided and profound faith that made life meaningful and death acceptable.[6]

Reimer later gives more details about this overall attitude towards life and death that existed in pre-modern times. He talks in great detail about how Judaism simultaneously had a vision of the beauty of the afterlife, but the emphasis is always on the here and now, living each moment until the moment of death. He states, "It is greater to struggle on earth, than to be an angel in heaven. Earthly life, mortal life, is precisely the arena where the covenant between God and man must be fulfilled."[7] How did Jews go from such a clear and trusting vision of God and life and death to our present relationship to death?

If we look at history, we see that during the times of the pogroms of Eastern Europe, Jews were forced to give up jobs that involved physical labor. In some areas, Jews were only allowed to be money collectors, or to serve in a narrow range of positions. From the twelfth through the twentieth century, the Jews of Europe regularly experienced vicious attacks. There were repeated rumors that the Jews had killed humans in sacrifice, even though this never happened and was strictly against the Jewish religion. The first charge of ritual murder was in 1147 in Norwich, England. Throughout this period, it was difficult for Jews to settle down, never knowing when their community might be attacked. Many people think that Jewish oppression centered on the Holocaust of the twentieth century, but similar oppression had gone on for hundreds of years.

Jews have had a history of persecution not only in the pogroms, but also in the Holocaust.

The Holocaust definitely plays a role in Jewish anxieties about health and death. For example, when I was in my early forties, I went through a period of being extremely worried about my health for no apparent reason. At the time, I was writing about the Holocaust, in which many of my grandparents' relatives had died in the concentration camps. In my family and in many Jewish families, the Holocaust is a historical ghost.[8] Having the Holocaust as a familial and cultural background has many unidentified effects. In my family, the ghost of the Holocaust contributed to a general anxious atmosphere. My family members seemed to feel insecure and had a vague sense that something was wrong. Since this anxiety was indistinct and formless, it was easy to somatize it and look for what might be wrong in our bodies. As I was writing about the Holocaust, I also found myself dreaming about it at night. The writing and the dreaming seemed cathartic, and the wave of anxiety I had been experiencing in relation to my health passed. At this point, I realized that I was experiencing the remnants of the Holocaust in my body, and that other family members must have felt similar feelings.

I have heard about other Jews who were similarly impacted. For example, one of my friends said that he could never trust the world after what the Holocaust had done to him and his family. This mistrust of the world and the environment easily leads to a generalized sense of insecurity, vulnerability, and worry about what might go wrong with the physical body.

In families where a great deal of anxiety is present, it may be helpful to bring up historical ghosts as a possible source of anxiety. In Chapter Ten, which addresses the stages of life, we will explore in great detail how to work with family ghosts that lurk behind anxieties around health and death.

I believe that the long-term intense restrictions and ongoing persecution caused a large-scale shift in collective Jewish culture. While Jewish culture had always valued learning and studying and the mind, it was also quite body-oriented. Jews were a people of the Earth whose holidays were based on harvests and other natural rhythms. It is highly possible that when we were forced off the land and allowed to work only in mental jobs, our relationships to our bodies changed. One sign of being disconnected from body awareness and experiences is that a person develops a more mental view that thinks and worries about body experience. Being forced up into our heads may have helped split Jews off from our bodies, turning the body into something to worry over rather than to experience.

While Jews have become disconnected and worried about the body, in other ways the connection with the body has always been there. The Jewish ancestors were farmers and shepherds who had strong connections with their bodies. Jewish spiritual traditions were open to sexuality, and even conveyed our love for the divine in sensual language, as in King Solomon's *Song of Songs*. This background has been covered up by years of oppression and cultural shifts, but is still apparent in that Judaism generally has a more open and positive view towards sexuality than many other religions. While Christianity contributed to the mind/body split by repressing sexuality and considering it evil, Judaism has conveyed a positive sense of the body in this area. In Judaism, connecting to oneself through sexuality has generally been supported. This may have been connected with a desire to support sex so that more children would be born and the

Jewish people would flourish. It may also be that the Jewish orientation toward healthy sexuality was simply too powerful to suppress as history moved forward. Rabbi Gershon Winkler, in his book *Sacred Secrets, The Sanctity of Sex in Jewish Law and Lore,* offers intriguingly interesting theories in this area. He says that Judaism had originally a most wholesome, positive view of sex, not only as procreation, but as enjoyment as well. His idea is that this changed, "only after centuries of subjection to host religions and cultures that all but squelched the notion of sensuality, often by death." Under such conditions, laws evolved in the Jewish codes that strove to parallel the sexual ethics of Jews with those of Christians, for example, so that the Jewish community would have one more ace in its survival cards."[9]

Rabbi Winkler quotes one of the greatest rabbinic scholars, the Ramban, on sex when he says, "No one should claim that sex is ugly or repulsive. God forbid. Sexual intercourse is called "knowing" in the Scriptures (Gen.4:1), and not in vain is it called thus…If we were to say that sex is repulsive, then we blaspheme God who created the genitals…. All body parts are neutral; the use we make of them determines whether they are holy or unholy."[10]

It is interesting that Freud, the first modern theorist who addressed the repression of sexuality, was Jewish. His method, psychoanalysis, largely focuses on helping people with the effects of repression. David Balkan, in *Sigmund Freud and the Jewish Mystical Tradition*, and Dennis Klein, in *Jewish Origins of the Psychoanalytic Movement*, both place Freud's work in the context of Judaism and relate his positions to Jewish mysticism These authors address the mystical Kabbalistic roots of Freud's work. They also place his work in a historical context, pointing out that while the entire culture was suffering from repression at this time in history, Jewish thinkers helped develop tools to fight against this growing repression.

Along these lines, it is also interesting to note the background climate in which Freud, a Jew, founded modern psychology. During Freud's time, sex was more repressed than in modern Jewish culture today, and Freud was quite clear about the relationship between repressing sexuality and the development of neuroses such as anxiety. Wilhelm Reich, another Jewish psychologist, was even more detailed about the negative impacts on the mind and body when people repress sexuality.

In my own life experience and experience working with clients, I have also noticed that repression of sexuality contributes to general anxiety. In most cases, if a person is able to open up sexually with an appropriate and satisfying partner, the person will not only be less anxious in general, but particularly less anxious about their health.

In his article, *No Trees Please, We're Jewish*[11] Andrew Furman provides a historical perspective on how many Jews have been cut off from nature. I believe that this distancing from nature is a predominant factor in losing faith in nature, and therefore in the body and its physical processes. Much of his article is based on the observation that few modern Jewish writers base their stories in nature; instead, most stories by modern Jewish writers are based in cities. Furman shows how Jews as a people started with a holy attitude towards nature. He cites the principle of baal tashkhit, the insistence on the preservation of nature, which is to be followed even in war. The *Talmud,* one of the books that record the Jewish oral tradition, says that scholars were told they should pray for the health of a sick tree. He quotes Deuteronomy, which forbids us to harm trees, even in war.

Furman provides several reasons for the distancing between Jews and nature. First, he cites the rationalist or Mitnagged tradition, from which many of the Ashkenazic Jewish American writers come. This tradition, which was at its height in the eighteenth century under the leadership of the great rabbi Vilna Goan, was a turning point in this shift away from nature. The rationalist tradition emphasized study and text as the place to worship God, rather than nature as where God was to be worshipped. Furman quotes Irving Howe, who said, "What linked man and God in our tradition was not nature but the commandment."[12] He also quotes one of the eminent rabbis of our time, Rabbi Joseph Soloveitchik, as saying that the religious person does not seek to be inspired by, or isn't even overly curious about, the natural world. The natural world is only to be viewed through the lenses of religious law.

Furman points out that the rabbinic tradition was worried that Jews would idolize nature and become pagans; therefore, the rationalistic tradition takes a hostile, antagonistic view towards nature. There are striking similarities in modern medicine, where rationalism has also found a home. Given its rationalistic approach, it is no wonder that modern medicine views nature as an enemy, rather than the Tao, or the direction, in which nature is trying to emerge. In addition, it is interesting to note that many modern Jewish doctors have turned to orthodoxy. Both modern medicine and Orthodox Judaism turn away from following nature and instead follow more rational approaches. Orthodox Judaism stresses a strict adherence to the laws specified in the Torah. These laws regulate all aspects of human behavior. According to the Orthodox Jews, it is through this strict observance of laws that people can fulfill God's commandments and wishes. While medicine and orthodoxy look very different from the outside, their core beliefs around rationality, law, and hostility to nature are very similar.

Both modern medicine and Orthodox Judaism take a hostile view of nature, assuming that it is not to be trusted; much of modern science talks of conquering nature. When we move from studying and celebrating nature to relying on formal knowledge, we marginalize the more mystical and dreamlike aspects of life. We become materialists—only studying and valuing what is right in front of us, whether it be the given text or the proven scientific data. The unknown, the mysterious, and the unpredictable are marginalized and feared. Rabbi Gershon Winkler illustrates this point by talking about how the laws regarding sex between a man and woman during menstruation, evolved. He says, of these times, "However, in examining the oppressive circumstances during the history of the era, we discover that the Jewish people in general were losing their connectedness with the earth and consequently with their bodies. This was an age during which this once earthy people were being deprived of their heritage of living on the land and of being attuned to Nature, both theologically and cosmologically.[13] He goes on to talk about how this split for earth consciousness was both one of sprit and of body.

For example, I recently met with the head physician of a large coma hospital. The other doctors hadn't informed him that I had worked with some of the coma patients there and achieved almost miraculous results with people who statistically were not supposed to improve. Despite these great improvements for patients, he insisted that I would not be allowed to work further with the patients. I heard from him the same rationalist view I have heard so many times. Despite the fact that positive changes were happening in front of his eyes, and despite the fact that he liked some of the ideas and liked me personally, he couldn't allow any method that was not supported by vast research.

I agreed with him that we needed to accumulate more data and prove the method in a linear, rational, accepted scientific mode. However, I also said that such research would take years, and that many of the people in his hospital would have to wait for years for a chance to experience positive changes. He said, "Yes, that was right." In this case, the method had become God.

Similarly, in Orthodox Judaism, the rules become a central part of the worship. Some people I know seem more concerned thinking about the rules than the God they are supposed to serve through the rules. Many doctors I have interacted with seem more concerned with the accepted forms than in what works for the individual person. For example, one of my clients had severe symptoms that she and I both believed came from her medication. The doctor said that it was impossible for the medication to create such side effects. Finally, the patient convinced the doctor to take her off the medication, and suddenly she felt much better.

In another example, a client had a brain tumor. The doctor removed it, and her symptoms increased. The doctor ran tests, took pictures, and told my client that it was rationally impossible for her symptoms to be increasing. Rationality, scientific tests, and hard data were his God. He wasn't interested in dreaming or in her process. When we worked on her symptoms, she stated that she knew the only change she still needed to make in her life was to separate from her husband, which she was terrified to do. I told her to imagine she was leaving him, and for the first time in six months, her head pain disappeared completely. She eventually left her husband, and still, many years later, her head pain has never returned.

In Orthodoxy, whether it is medical or religious, there is a rigid need to follow absolute standards that the individual cannot modify. Both modern medicine and Orthodox Judaism define reality, be it material or spiritual, in a very fixed way. It is also interesting to note that both modern medicine and Orthodox Judaism have evolved from more mystical traditions into their current rigid forms. For example, modern medicine developed from ancient Greek healing traditions that included going to a cave and praying for guidance about a patient's healing. The caduceus, which is the snake on the staff symbol of modern medicine, originates from this tradition. Similarly, Orthodox Judaism came from a tradition of visionaries, prophets, and wild dreamers. Both traditional medicine and Orthodox Judaism have stepped away from the circle of nature into a linear approach to achieving medical or religious ends.

Religious Views That Alleviate Anxiety

Growing up as a reform Jew, I learned very little about death. I heard that people went to heaven to be with God, which sounded nice, but it didn't help me with my anxiety on earth. My Christian friends also talked about the rewards of the afterlife, but I was looking for relief here and now. Eventually, I found what I was looking for could be found in Jewish mysticism.

One of the most famous Jewish mystics was Isaac Luria, who belonged to the Kabbalists, a group of Jewish mystics from Safed, in what is now Israel. Luria and his followers focused particularly on the concept of the transmigration of souls.

Part of this theory is that souls are reincarnated. Similar to a concept in Buddhism, each soul was considered to have a goal of ending the repetitive cycle of death and rebirth in the physical world.[14]

The Kabbalah also contains a similar concept to the Buddhist bodhisattva, which is the concept that some souls, even after they have freed themselves from the wheel of reincarnation, decide to return to earth as a service to others. Edward Hoffman noted that

> The Kabbalists have regarded such figures as making the ultimate sacrifice to raise up their fellow human beings—to come back to our corporal world, with all of its despair and disorder, after having tasted the inexpressible delights of the World of the Spirit. The sixteenth century mystic Solomon Alkabez describes such souls as "those who return not on account of their having omitted a religious duty, let alone for having committed a trespass, but solely out of compassion with their contemporaries."[15]

Among the Kabbalists of Safed, particularly in the 1600's, trying to identify who knew whom from previous incarnations was a common activity. Hoffman points out that focus on the immortal soul has greatly declined in Modern Judaism, but it was a central part of early Jewish mysticism. The main theme was that each soul returns to earth to complete its tasks; therefore, each person has a unique mission that must be fulfilled through reincarnation until complete.

Hoffman also talks about the mystics' emphasis on dying consciously, and Kabbalist tradition contains many stories of masters who died in states of great peace and bliss. The *Zohar*, one of the main texts of Kabbalist thought, speaks of death as a doorway to other dimensions, and considers that there is continuity of consciousness between worlds. Another text, the *Book of Splendor*, talks about death as a time of experiencing the presence of loved ones who have already died and of being bathed in a brilliant light. These descriptions are similar to those found in modern books such as Dr. Raymond Moody's, *Life After Life, The Integration of a Phenomenon—Survival of Bodily Death*, and *The Light Beyond*.

In his book, *Jewish Reflections on Death*, Jack Reimer talks about the death of many of these great mystics. He says that the Ari, one of the great Kabbalists, told his followers that he would continue to teach them after he died. When a rabbi asked him how he would continue to help them with the spiritual practices after he had departed from the world, he said, "I myself shall come and teach you. It is not for you to delve into secret things, how I shall come—whether by night or by day, or in a vision."[16]

Reimer also talks about the death of Rebbe Nachman, a great mystic and the grandson of the Bal Shem Tov, the founder of Hasidism. When it appeared that he had died, his followers said, "Our Rabbi—with whom have you left us?" It is said that he raised his head and his face, as if to say, "I am not leaving you." He then died.[17]

Integrating the Kabbalah's Teachings Lessens Anxiety

The more I learned about the Kabbalah and other mystical traditions, the more at peace I felt. All of these traditions embrace the central principle that in death, something dies and something else goes on. These ideas fit with my own experiences of people who have died. For example, the first two people that I was close to who died, were a close friend of mine in high school and an uncle who died while I was in college. My friend died in an auto accident, while my uncle, who had been in good health, died instantly of a heart attack. The night before each person died, I had a dream about the death. In each case, I was only partially shocked when my parents told me the news. Experiences such as these and others I have had in dreamwork, bodywork, and meditation make me believe that death is in the realm of the eternal.

In many cultures around the world, reincarnation is considered a normal part of everyday life. I spent time with one group of people in the Middle East who told me that children regularly take their parents to a neighbor's house to show them where they buried things in their previous life. In such cultures, death is part of an ongoing process of life that continues past the point of death. In contrast, for those of us who are Jews and / or Western people, when we block access to our mystical teachers, and to the mystics in us, death and life are full of anxiety.

One of the life experiences that have caused me the most anxiety is the loss of important relationships, such as the one I lost when I separated from a long-term partner. The Kabbalistic view that we will finish our work with those we are intimate with over the course of many lifetimes both gave me hope and lessened my anxiety. While it is important to do everything one can in a lifetime, sometimes a person can only go so far. It is comforting to think that perhaps the rest will be worked out later in this life, or in the next life. When I think of all I want to accomplish and experience in this life, it is reassuring to know that there may be other opportunities in other lifetimes. The vision of dying and being met by loved ones while immersed in glowing light is far more comforting than a vision of dying alone in a sterile hospital setting and not going on past the point of death.

Anxiety about health and dying may serve in part to guide us toward a more mystical view of life. Jewish mysticism provides a perspective that life and death are full of meaning; thus, it may offer relief for some of the anxiety that we suffer in our modern world.

Summary

In modern life, Jews have been increasingly cut off from our roots in nature and our mystical teachings, which may well have contributed to our anxiety about illness and death. By reconnecting with nature, sexuality, and mysticism, we reconnect with our bodies and spirits. From this perspective, illness and death are a natural part of life, and are thus less terrifying. Spiritual powers often terrorize us until we get closer to them and can understand and identify with them. At this point, we are on a path that can lead us to the full consciousness in life and death that is a central topic of mysticism.

EXERCISE: Inner work exercise.

1. Spend some time thinking and writing about historical ghosts that may have influenced your family. What is your cultural background? Could there be unprocessed issues around slavery, the holocaust, the taking of Native American land by European invaders, the internment of Japanese in camps in the United States during World War II, or other historical events? How have these events influenced your level of anxiety in

general? Speculate about how this may have influenced your feelings about health and death issues.

2. Take some time to meditate. Experiment with making your mind open and unknowing. Next, take some time to visualize yourself dying. Imagine that when you die, you will meet loved ones and be bathed in light. See if you can visualize being surrounded by loved ones and light at this moment.

3. What is your experience like in doing this? Compare this experience to your normal feelings when you think about dying.

4. Think of a life problem or relationship that you have been struggling with. Imagine that you have many lifetimes to work on this issue. Do you feel differently about the problem if you imagine you have lifetimes to work on it, and that there is no rush?

5. Imagine that you might die tomorrow. Is there anything you want to do or work on right now?

6. See if you can identify with a something larger than yourself, something eternal, which contains both kinds of awareness around this life problem or relationship problem.[18] This larger thing is aware of both the limited and eternal parts of Yourself. Try picking a specific problem and both imagining that you may die tomorrow, and how will this change you, and that you have an eternity to resolve this problem. Notice what it is like to contain all of this awareness.

CHAPTER 3

Zen Buddhism

Zen Buddhism has generated tremendous interest in the West, partially due to the wisdom this approach brings to the area of death and dying. Like the work of the Kabbalists, Zen wakes us up to our limited view of death and dying. Whole books have been written on this aspect of Zen; my purpose in this chapter is to focus specifically on how Zen concepts can help us to deal with our anxieties in these areas.[19]

Zen Views, Western Views

Philip Kapleau summarizes the basic Zen attitude towards death as follows: "Beings come and go, but the flame of life, the generating impulse animating all existences and underlying the whole of creation, neither comes and goes, it burns eternally, with no beginning, with no end."[20] Kapleau contrasts this attitude with the Western approach to death, in which death is an enemy that needs to be overcome. He notes that, "Death, which ought to be welcomed as natural and inevitable, becomes the Grim Reaper; and dying the terror of all terrors."[21]

In Zen philosophy, death is seen as a natural part of the circle of life and death. From this perspective, only part of us dies. One main focus in Zen is learning to identify with the eternal part that lives on eternally.

Kapleau tells a story about the great Zen Master Dogo. In the tale, a student goes with the master to offer condolences to a family that has just lost a loved one. The student asks the master if the person in the coffin is alive or dead. The master says, "I won't say alive and I won't say dead." The student becomes so upset that he threatens to hit the master if he will not give an answer, and the master again says that he won't say one or the other. At this moment the student had a deep insight into the nature of life and death. One of the main goals of Zen is to be free from the dualistic thinking of life and death; therefore, Master Dogo cannot say alive or dead because he no longer perceives death and life as separate. They are intimately related to, and part of, each other.

Zen Masters at the Moment of Death

When a Zen master has gone beyond experiencing life and death as a duality, the moment of death is often experienced with laughter, smiling, or meditation. The master has already gone beyond attachment to the present physical life. For example, Zen master Takkan's students begged him for some last words. He finally died after he wrote the word "dream." A goal of Zen is to be able to connect with that dreamlike place from which life and death arise, a place of oneness.

In Zen philosophy, people are born and reborn to work out our karma. From this perspective, dying is not much different than getting on a jet and starting over in a new country in a new time zone. Zen also talks about the momentary flow of living and dying as change at every moment. At the cellular level, while a person is alive, cells are constantly dying and being reborn. Thus, even in death, a part of oneself remains. Zen master Ikkyu says on his deathbed, "I shan't die, I shan't go anywhere, I'll be here. But don't ask me anything, I shan't answer."[22]

Zen and the Fear of Death

Kapleau quotes Lyall Watson on the fear of death: "In cultures where death is dealt with more openly and seen as part of the living process there is no fear of death."[23] Kapleau takes the view that a certain amount of fear of death is natural, and even helpful, since it can serve to awaken people to their true nature and keep them from unnecessary or foolish risks. While some fear of death is natural, Kapleau addresses the paralyzing anxiety that many people in the West feel about death. He quotes French psychotherapist Ignance Lepp, whose research indicated that those individuals most dedicated to living fully are least afraid of dying. In Lepp's words, "It is my conviction that an intense love of life is the best and perhaps only effective antidote against the fear of death."[24]

Kapleau notes that in cultures where community focus is more important than focus on the individual, death anxieties are greatly lessened. For Zen Buddhists, part of living fully and loving life involves overcoming the limitations of the individual ego, since the ego is seen to lead people into the land of duality, where death and life are not one. Anxiety, especially about death, comes about because our ego keeps us from experiencing our real Self. We live in our intellect, which constantly divides our experience into good and bad, life and death, illness and health. Only through reconnecting with our true Self can we connect with the enlightened part of ourselves that is beyond fears of death. In Buddhism, all people are potentially capable of reaching enlightenment, in which we can see that living and dying, and all other distinctions are part of a dream. Kapleau says it so beautifully—

Bravely let go of your hold
On the edge of the precipice
And die to the small self.
Then what is naturally revealed
Is the True-nature in which
There is neither life nor death.[25]

The Zen Emphasis on Life

In Zen, the focus is on life, rather than on death. The world is experienced as an awesome place, and each moment is the eternal moment, to be lived fully. One great master dies while commenting on how wonderful the cake he just ate tasted. If one lives fully in every moment until death, then death is just one more experience of life, not a fear or tragedy to be avoided.

One way to work on one's death is to live fully. In my personal life, I have started to live more fully by shifting my emphasis from fears of dying to living fully, finding where I inhibit myself, and where I want to be more free. Writing this book has been yet another step on this path of liberation. By meditating on and writing about death, I feel gradually ever freer. When I first started writing on this topic, I feared that writing a book on dying might take me back into the anxious states I had previously experienced. To my delight, the more I wrote and meditated, the freer I felt. This experience suggests two main directions of dealing with death anxieties. One direction is to live fully in the present, to see life as an amazing blessing, and to drink it up. A complementary direction is to meditate on death, impermanence, and the eternal, and to reach a place in one's consciousness where life and death spring from the same well.

The Work of Stephen Levine

Stephen Levine is one individual who has done a great deal to raise Western awareness around death. In Who Dies? Levine expresses his teachings, which have been influenced by his study of Zen. Levine writes

> There seems to be much less suffering for those who live life in the wholeness that includes death. Not a morbid preoccupation with death but rather a staying in the loving present, a life that focuses on each precious moment. I see few whose participation in life has prepared them for death. Few who have explored their heart and mind as perfect preparation for whatever might come next be it death or sickness, grief or joy.
>
> Who is prepared to die? Who has lived so fully that they are not threatened by their imaginings of nonexistence? For it is only the idea of death that frightens us. It is the unknown we pull back from.[26]

Like the Buddhist masters, Levine talks about the wisdom of impermanence. What makes us fear dying? It is our sense of ourselves as fixed, that there is an identity, or "I," that doesn't change. However, this is a set-up for terrible anxiety, for who we are constantly changes as our outer and inner lives change. Levine goes on to talk about how if we don't jump into this ever-changing river of life, we miss living while fearing dying. He says, "To become wholly born, we must stop postponing life. To the degree that we postpone life, we postpone death. We deny death and life in one fell swoop."[27]

Levine points out that fears of death and of life are intimately linked. He says, "Our fear of death is directly equitable to our fear of life. When we think of dying, we think of losing something called "me."[28] Levine talks about the same ideas that are central to Zen, i.e., that the fear of death is based on the fear of losing the part of us we identify as "I". We are afraid to die into our bigger selves. Levine says it most clearly when he says, "What was your face before you were born? Who you are, in reality, was never born and never dies. Let go of who you think you are and become who you have always been."[29]

This is one of the clearest statements I have found about how to connect with one's eternal nature and thus alleviate some of the potentially crippling anxiety around death. Levine goes further in his discussion of how to deal with the fears that keep us disconnected from life. He says, "all these states of mind which we fear so much can actually be mulched back into ourselves to become fertilizer, the manure for further growth. Which means that in order to allow these materials to compost, to become rich fertilizers for growth, we must begin to make room in our hearts of ourselves."[30] Levine refers to our Oneness, who we are past the small "me". The small "me" pushes out so much of our experience that it cuts us off from life, while the bigger view makes space for the fearful parts as well. In this openness of relating to our whole Selves, fear becomes part of the material that is our whole being, and our whole Self can deal with the fear. It recycles fear and recasts it into a new configuration of facing all of life and death. Fear itself transforms, and as we transform, we transform our fears.

Summary

Many people, in the East and the West, turn to Zen, in part because it offers relief from our chronic dualistic thinking, which creates internal conflict and anxiety. Zen masters provide a great model for living and dying fully, without fear. For the Zen master, there is no separation between living and dying. Death and life happen at every moment, and death is viewed as a natural transition.

Zen is about living fully in the moment. Sometimes meditating on death helps one develop the detachment to live this way. Without seeing life and death as connected, one can easily be terrified by life and by death.

To be free of fears of death requires moving past the ego and its reliance on intellect, and learning to connect with the Self that is beyond individual ego. This leads us to an eternal sense of life, where it is possible to face death and life with great inner peace and freedom.

Stephen Levine presents Zen concepts in terms that are clear and relevant to those from a Western background.

EXERCISE: Finding Your Internal Zen Master

1. Find a place where you can sit and meditate. Let your mind relax and open. Imagine that you have died, and a part of you could look down and see yourself from above after your death.

2. Notice your spontaneous reaction—do you cry, laugh, do nothing?

3. Imagine letting the part of yourself that is watching could interact with the self on earth that has died. Imagine that your dead body and the other dead part

of you watching from above could both speak. Let a dialogue unfold between them.

4. Try seeing the whole drama as a dream.
5. Experiment with making poetry or music or a song about this experience, even if you don't think of yourself as poetic or musical.
6. Imagine thinking that all of these parts, the dead one and the one talking to the dead, and the you who you are right now, are part of the whole that you are?

| CHAPTER 4 |

Tibetan Buddhism

My religion is to live—and die—without regret. – Tibetan poet saint Milarepa[31]

Tibetan Buddhism offers one of the most elaborate views of the dying process. For those people who feel less anxious about new journeys when they have information about the place and a map of the territory, the Tibetan Buddhist path may offer relief from death anxieties. Like Zen, it is rooted in the deep belief that death is a natural state. Tibetan Buddhism adds to other concepts we have seen thus far by showing us how we can actually prepare for death.

A central concept in Tibetan Buddhism is that whatever one experiences in one's consciousness in life is what they will experience in dying and the afterlife. Therefore, it is important to develop one's awareness, which will help a person have a peaceful death. In Tibetan Buddhism, one develops consciousness both through living life in a virtuous way and through meditation practices, some of which focus on preparing for death. Phowa training, which teaches people how to merge their individual consciousness with the pure essential energy of the universe, is one of the most critical meditations for all people. People can visualize their energy merging with any of the images they hold sacred, such as Buddha, Jesus, or other images of the divine source of all being.

The Tibetan system also describes in detail the different stages of the afterlife. It helps us prepare for them in advance and to move through them as they progress. This approach provides a practical training for death. In Tibetan Buddhist theory, these practices can even help those who have already died if those who remain practice them for the person who has died. This concept provides reassurance that a relationship exists between those who are living and those who have already died; not only are we not alone after death, but we can reach our loved ones with our love, energy and healing after they die. Tibetan Buddhism offers a way to make living and dying a unified spiritual practice.

In the previous chapter, we took a brief look at Zen Buddhism; now we will visit Tibetan Buddhist theory as it relates to living and dying. There are many philosophical similarities between Zen and Tibetan Buddhism. We will find some of the main differences as we look at the Tibetan practice of working directly with the moment of death and the period just after a person dies. Tibetan Buddhism, like Zen, emphasizes death as a reality that can help wake people up to the here and now. In addition, Tibetan Buddhism makes a unique contribution to working with death and dying by preparing people for what they will need to do after they die.

Through providing training about how to face death, Tibetan Buddhism can help an individual feel empowered. We have seen that Zen and other theories help empower people to live fully, to be fully present at the moment of death, and to believe that they will likely return to earth for further development. Tibetan Buddhism teaches these same tenets; in addition, it teaches people who believe in reincarnation how to deal with the time period between the moment of death and rebirth. This information often seems to help people feel more empowered, because they have the skills to take an active role in their passage through the dying experience and the time following it.

A Brief Overview of Tibetan Buddhist Philosophy

With Tibetan Buddhism, as with other philosophies about living and dying, there is space here only for the briefest overview. For those who are interested in further exploration of Tibetan Buddhism, Sogyal Rinpoche's *The Tibetan Book of Living and Dying* is an excellent source.[32] Rinpoche echoes points we have seen in Zen Buddhism by pointing out that death is a natural part of life, and should be addressed as such. In Tibetan Buddhist tradition, children aren't protected from knowing about the reality of death; experiencing what happens when a person dies is considered an important part of life. In many Eastern perspectives, and particularly in Tibetan Buddhism, death is a natural part of life, and is neither sought after nor avoided. For people who fear death, viewing death as a part of nature can make it seem less frightening. If we can really trust nature, it is easier to trust the dying process, since the deep wisdom of nature is behind it. This perspective may be particularly helpful to people from a Western background, since in the typical Western perspective, death is a defeat to be avoided at all costs. Rinpoche notes that Westerners don't consider death an ordinary part of life; rather, we take one of two attitudes: "One [attitude] views death as something to scurry away from and the other as something that will just take care of itself. How far they both are from understanding death's true significance!"[33] To the Tibetan Buddhists, how our mind views something is very important. Rinpoche suggests that the right frame of mind relative to death is a combination of a spiritual and practical approach—one should neither deny death, nor ignore it, but should be aware of it as a natural part of life. If a person is interested in raising awareness of death as a natural part of life, I recommend that they regularly remind themselves that they will die someday. Next, they can ask themselves what they are doing in their consciousness to prepare for the inevitable and natural death that will come.

Rinpoche also makes a fascinating connection between the Western disconnection from the reality of death and our brutal destruction of the environment. In my own practice and life, I have noticed that people who have been anxious about death have found their worries decreasing when they work to support environmental causes. People in general feel better if they have a cause greater than themselves to connect with. Working for the environment can be particularly effective at relieving anxieties about dying, since the environment will survive beyond any individual's life; in working to protect it, we are thinking about many generations beyond our own.

For example, during a time when I was particularly anxious about my own health, I decided to organize a town meeting on a pressing environmental issue in my area. Almost immediately, I was greatly relieved from my health anxieties. This is the flip side of the connection that Rinpoche explains so clearly: "if disconnection from death leads to environmental destruction, embracing life and not denying death leads to awareness of and care for the environment. If I marginalize my awareness of death, then the death of the bigger physical environment is also of minimal concern. Awareness of my own death makes me aware of how I treat the earth, and makes me aware of how important it is that the earth survive. If I turn off awareness of death, not only I, but also all that is around me suffers. If I face my death, then all that is around me becomes part of me; I cannot turn my back on any of it. To face death is to face life, and to embrace death is to embrace all of life."

For example, when I couldn't face my own death, I couldn't face and feel the pain of environmental destruction. Years ago, when my neighbor cut down a beautiful forest to raise money for a good cause, I could not bear to see it. I fought the cutting, was able to preserve a bit of the land, but I never went back to see the place. Now that I have faced my own death, I could face the cut land and feel its agony. I no longer need to avoid environmental destruction because it reminds me of my own death. From my experience, I can suggest that one way to work on one's own anxieties about death is to be more connected to the physical earth and the environment, and to see how it feels to direct one's concerns and love towards the earth. It is quite likely to relieve anxiety about death and dying.

Both Zen and Tibetan Buddhism stress the wisdom that comes from embracing the impermanence of life. Opening up to the transitory nature of life helps us value and embrace life. When we live life fully, with full consciousness that we will die, death becomes a natural part of life. From this perspective, there is no need to spend a great deal of time worrying; there is too much to do in life, too much potential development before death occurs. By accepting change in life, we learn to let go and accept whatever happens. Letting go and accepting what comes one's way is like a small death—our sense of control and of knowing what will come die. Through training oneself to accept these small deaths, anxiety about death itself can be lessened. Training for death is like training for a marathon. One way to train is simply to worry about the inevitability of the upcoming event. A better way is to run a bit further every year, whether it is with one's awareness or one's body, so that one is ready when the big event comes along.

Tibetan Buddhism specifically addresses the importance of letting go, and talks about following a path of non-attachment. Through practicing meditation over a lifetime, Tibetan Buddhists practice letting go and gaining detachment. As one practices detachment, as the ego dissolves, one gains the security of being part of one great whole, and a hopeful attitude about death often emerges. As we embrace our death, and accept the truth of impermanence, we can find amazing freedom and peace. Sogyal Rinpoche quotes the Tibetan poet Milarepa when he says,

> In horror of death I took to the mountains—
> Again and again I meditated on the
> uncertainty of the hour of death,
> Capturing the fortress of the deathless
> unending nature of mind.
> Now all fear of death is over and done.[34]

The Tibetan Buddhists have specific meditation techniques that they practice. In my opinion, the method one chooses is not as important as having a means to work on oneself. What is important is that people pick some form of inner work to get to know their own minds better, and to take time to reflect on the meaning of their life and their death. This reflection itself can connect people to deeper levels of living, so that life becomes more meaningful, and death becomes part of life. The ordinary mind has trouble perceiving this, while a meditative mind can help us to be aware of this.

Bardo States

> We have seen that a central concept in Tibetan Buddhism is that death is natural. Since life and death are part of the same cycle, a person can use death to help with life, and use life to

> prepare for death. The Tibetan system divides life and death into four realities called bardos and offers guidance through each of the stages. By thinking about these stages, we can think more about how to live and die, and to prepare for death. The bardos are: the natural bardo of life, the painful bardo of dying, the luminous bardo of dharmana, and the karmic bardo of becoming. These four stages correspond to the bardo of this life, the bardo of dying, the bardo of dharmjatat or after death, and the bardo of rebirth. The bardo teachings believe in the importance of preparing for death. Sogyal Rinpoche says that, "For someone who has prepared and practiced, death comes not as a defeat but as a triumph, the crowning and most glorious moment in life."[35]

Most Westerners who know something about Tibetan Buddhism assume that the bardo states happen only after death, but the first bardo state actually lasts from the moment of birth to the moment of death. The other three bardo states happen after death. Tibetan Buddhism can help us fear death less if we think about having tastes of the all the bardo states during life, particularly in sleeping and dreaming. Going to sleep is related to the bardo of dying, dreaming to the bardo of becoming, and the luminous bardo to the time between falling asleep and beginning to dream. The luminous bardo involves the radiant states of clear light after death, which manifests as sound, color, and light. Because this is the after life step between death and rebirth, Rinpoche says that it corresponds to that part of sleep between falling asleep and before dreaming begins. We can prepare for our "big death" by experiencing the little death of dream and sleep states. Rinpoche says that by working with these various sleep states, we can practice and develop skills for the bardo states that occur from death on. He says, "What a real practitioner seeks to do is to keep, unfailing and unbroken, his or her awareness of the nature of mind throughout day and night, and so use directly the different phases of sleep and dream to recognize and become familiar with what will happen in the bardos during and after death."[36]

Years ago I heard Tibetan Lama Gyatryl Rinpoche say that Tibetan dream yoga was about being fully conscious at night, and also about seeing all of waking life as a dream. Dream yoga is a method of maintaining one's awareness while in dreaming, and becoming increasingly lucid, aware, and able to consciously interact and take action in one's dreams. Dream yoga also involves utilizing the dreaming states and sleep states to go into deeper and deeper states of awareness and consciousness. If we can be aware in these dream states, we can use them for training grounds for the states after death. It is like going to soccer practices before a big game. While practice is not the same, the preparation can help tremendously when you get in a tricky moment. Rinpoche says meditation is like daytime soccer practice, and sleep and dream yoga like a nighttime practice.

Rinpoche gives many techniques for helping people die peacefully; these techniques are also generally useful for lessening fear. They include helping people complete unfinished business, creating an atmosphere as beautiful and healing as possible, treating the dying person with great love and compassion, and guiding the person through coma and near death states.

One of the most important Tibetan Buddhist teachings to prepare for death is phowa practice. This practice is based on transforming individual energy by merging with the universal energy of one's Buddha nature. The practitioner learns to eject their consciousness at the moment of death, and merge it with the wisdom mind of Buddha. Rinpoche says that no matter what your spiritual tradition, you can at the moment of death "invoke wholeheartedly all the Buddha's and your master. Pray that, through regretting all your negative actions in this and other lives, they may be purified, and that you may die consciously and at peace, gain a good rebirth, and ultimately achieve liberation."[37] In phowa practice, one calls in the deepest spiritual parts of oneself and one's beliefs; next, the person asks that everything hurtful from this and other lives be purified; at this point, a person can die fully conscious and go further down the path to enlightenment.

Tibetan Buddhists and others who complete the Tibetan Buddhist training often appear to have a peaceful death. Perhaps people in the West would fear death less if we had a practice that helped us know what to do as we were dying. Many Tibetan Buddhists recommend phowa training to everyone, regardless of their religious persuasion, since it can positively transform the dying experience.

Another wonderful teaching from Tibetan Buddhism is its instructions on how to be with a person who has already died. Sogyal Rinpoche notes that the single most important thing one can do for someone who has died is the phowa practices, which can be done for others as well as for oneself. If someone doesn't know the practice, they can say a mantra or other holy words. It is especially important to send loving feelings and thoughts and to pray for those that have died. He also says it helps to do good work in their name, such as donating to charity, sponsoring spiritual retreats, or other acts of giving. Rinpoche says that the living can dedicate all the merit that comes from any act of kindness and generosity to those that have died.[38]

Similarly, Rinpoche says that people who have died are seven times more clairvoyant than when alive, so it is very important to be aware of one's behavior in order not to hurt them. For example, fighting over the dead person's possessions can bring them great pain.[39] In Tibetan Buddhist tradition, in addition to doing phowa for a person who has died, the living read to the dead from the *Tibetan Book of the Dead*. They also do the Ne Dren, the ritual for guiding the dead, or the Chang Chok, the ritual purification. Another practice done is the purification of the six realms, which is used to purify the six negative emotions. The living also do a practice on the hundred peaceful and wrathful deities. In this meditation, the practitioner imagines sending out deities who send rays of light to the dead and purify their negative karma or deeds. In Tibetan Buddhist tradition, weekly practices are done for seven weeks for the person who has died in order to help them go through the different bardo states. Shamanistic approaches, as well as Judaism and many other spiritual traditions, also include rituals that not only heal the grief of those of us left behind, but also help the person who is in other realms.

Summary

We have seen that Tibetan Buddhism offers both a philosophy and practices for how to prepare for death. Death is seen as terrifying largely because it is denied, made to seem unnatural, and not prepared for. Therefore, Tibetan Buddhists emphasize teaching about death as a natural process. These teachings help us face and prepare for death, therefore greatly reducing our fears of the unknown.

| CHAPTER 5 |

Shamanism and Personal Power

The term shamanism refers to a combination of healing, spiritual, artistic, and community living practices common in many indigenous cultures.

As a general rule, in indigenous cultures that practice shamanism as a guiding part of their spiritual, healing, and community life, death is much more visible and openly addressed than in Western culture. Many shamanic cultures have rituals, such as Mexico's Day of the Dead that help people maintain relationships with those who have died. Some Native American cultures burn food and blankets to take care of the dead. Carlos Casteneda, an anthropologist who wrote about his encounters with the powerful Yaqui Indian shaman Don Juan, has helped bring the teaching of shamanism to the Western world. In this chapter, I will focus largely upon his work to illustrate how shamanism can help alleviate anxiety about illness and death.[40]

The Role of Death in Life

In his encounters with Don Juan, Carlos gets frequent lessons about death. In *The Power of Silence*, Don Juan teaches Carlos about the central role death plays on every shaman's path. Don Juan's talks about death as follows:

The idea of death therefore is of monumental importance in the life of a sorcerer. I have shown you innumerable things about death to convince you that the knowledge of our impending and unavoidable end is what gives us sobriety. Our most costly mistake as average men is indulging in a sense of immortality. It is as though we believe that if we don't think about death we can protect ourselves from it.[41]

Carlos begins to argue with him, saying that it is better not to think about death in order not to worry about it. At that moment, Carlos serves as the voice of western rationalism, which deals with fear by attempting to avoid it.

Don Juan gives a startling answer, saying that avoiding awareness of our death may reduce fear, but only at great cost. He says that:

> Without a clear view of death, there is no order, no sobriety, no beauty. Sorcerers[42] struggle to gain this crucial insight in order to help them realize at the deepest possible level that they have no assurance whatsoever that their lives will continue beyond the moment. That realization gives sorcerers the courage to be patient—and yet take action, courage to be acquiescent without being stupid.[43]

Don Juan goes on to talk about the courage that comes from facing death. It is interesting to note that his goal is not to remove fear, but to gain the qualities of sobriety and courage that come from having full awareness of one's death. Don Juan points out that consciousness of impending death gives people the courage to act as spiritual warriors without becoming self- important.

Carlos is not convinced that facing death will do anything other than make him depressed, and he refers to death as an enemy. Don Juan counters with his opinion that death is our challenger, not our enemy. He says that people are essentially passive until the point that they feel pressured by death. He says that there are two options: death can push us until we break and it triumphs, or we can somehow defeat death. In his words, "Sorcerers defeat death and death acknowledges the defeat by letting the sorcerer go free, never to be challenged again."[44]

Carlos asks if this means that sorcerers become immortal. Don Juan says absolutely not; rather, it means that they take a "somersault into the inconceivable."[45] In other words, we break out of the limits of our perception. Once we have defeated death, we are free to perceive reality in new ways; free of our old conceptions and patterns.

At one point in Carlo's early training, Don Juan tells Carlos what it means to live and integrate death while being alive. He tells him that, "You are dead. The sorcerers' grand trick, however, is to be aware that they are dead. Their ticket to impeccability must be wrapped in awareness."[46]

Don Juan makes several other profound points in his education of Casteneda. He distinguishes between denying death and using death to give yourself a jolt to awaken. He also points out that death is a motivator that pushes us to make something of our lives and that awareness of death can take us beyond ordinary reality and the limits of our perception. You may have noticed that Don Juan echoes the Buddhist views on the wisdom of impermanence. As we move further into our exploration of various views of death, we will find that people all over the world have come to similar conclusions about how to work with death, including this concept of remembering the impermanence of life.

Death Itself

In *The Active Side of Infinity,* his final work, Casteneda writes about what may happen after death, based on what he has learned from Don Juan. Casteneda brings up the fascinating concept that we may have some choice around what happens when we die. Don Juan notes that sorcerers, through using their awareness during the dying process, had discovered the following information. First, at the moment of death, the sorcerers saw a "dark sea of awareness sucking in...the awareness of living creatures."[47] Then, if a sorcerer had done a thorough accounting of his or her life, "the dark sea of awareness took their awareness in the form of their life experiences, but didn't touch their life force. Sorcerers had found out a gigantic truth about the forces of the universe: The dark sea of awareness wants only our life experiences, not our life Force."[48]

This learning on the part of the sorcerers is similar to the Tibetan Buddhist teaching that individuals who are able to let go of their personal selves and merge with the great life energy can choose whether or not to be reborn. These individuals have more choice than the person with an average level of awareness, who is automatically reborn after death.

Process-Oriented Psychology has come to a similar perspective via another route. Let's think about the course of a human life. A person is born, grows up, and begins to accumulate various experiences. Gradually, the person begins to identify with these experiences. Particularly if the experiences are traumatic, a person may begin to see him or herself largely as a victim of the experiences. Then, if a person works through the experience, it no longer has the same hold on them—their identity expands and they spend less time thinking about or identifying with the experience.

We can all think of times we have identified with our experiences in daily life. For example, we get upset with someone. We walk around in a state of being "not-quite-all-here." We think about what happened in the past, what to say in the future. Finally, we talk to the person we are upset with, work it all out, and feel much lighter. If you do this with all the major situations in your life, when you die, there is no past to grab at you. You have immense freedom to be in the present.

Process Work calls this progressive letting go of identifying with experience "erasing personal history". If one is able to let go of attachment to personal experience, one is able to identify not only with the little you, but also with the Big You. The Big You contains your whole self and is serves as a connection point to whole universe, which is unfolding through you. From this perspective, you can see yourself both as a microcosm of the universe, and as part of the whole universe's unfolding.

If we look back now at Don Juan, we might see that erasing personal history means that the "dark sea of awareness" does not need to take you in to wipe the slate clean. If we erase our personal history, the slate is already clean. If your slate is clean, the life force remains with you, rather than returning to the "dark sea of awareness." Don Juan says that death disintegrates an ordinary person, but for the sorcerer, death is a unifying force. The awareness of the sorcerer survives as long as the earth exists, because the sorcerer is transformed into basic life energy. Therefore, sorcerers do achieve something like immortality.

Casteneda prescribes a method he calls *recapitulation* to cleanse one's slate. Recapitulation involves going over all the memories of one's life in order to re-experience them in a way that combines the experience with the detachment and awareness that wasn't present the first time these things happened. We have seen a similar prescription in the Zen suggestion that in order to live life fully, one should die in life before one really dies.

Casteneda's theoretical framework can help reduce anxiety about death by helping people see death as a challenger rather than as an enemy. He helps us prepare for death by recapitulating, or cleaning our slates; he also introduces the possibility of reaching a state of awareness that transcends the power of death itself.

Summary

We have seen that in general, shamanic cultures have more relationship to death and those who have died than Western cultures do. In the specific teachings of the Yaqui shaman, Don Juan, we saw that death can serve as a challenger that snaps us out of our passivity towards life. We also saw that cleaning the slate of one's person history introduces the possibility of achieving a state of great freedom upon dying.

EXERCISE: Death as an Awakening Force

1. Try imagining for a moment that your death is coming soon, but you don't know when. How much time you have may depend on the way in which you live your

life, and on how much awareness and energy you bring to your remaining days.

2. What kind of changes would you make in how you live daily? What kind of passivity might you shed?
3. Write down some of these changes, and think about what ones you may want to integrate in your daily life.

EXERCISE: Reaching Freedom

1. Sit quietly and put your mind in a meditative state. Now, review your life, noting which memories stick with and disturb you.
2. Recall one of the situations you remember in detail. Let whatever feelings and thoughts come up emerge, and try to express them now in whatever way suits you. Keep doing this and notice when you begin to feel lighter.
3. Staying with your feelings of lightness, try to express them through art, poetry, music, dance, or any other form.
4. To finish, try to find a movement that reminds you of this lightness. The next time you find yourself in a heavy situation, make this movement and recall this state of lightness. See how this affects you—are you swallowed up by the situation, or do you find some freedom and choice that you might not previously have had?

| CHAPTER 6 |

Process-Oriented Psychology

Process-Oriented Psychology, a western psychological approach, has much in common with the eastern and shamanic traditions that we have seen thus far. In the spirit of Zen and Tibetan Buddhism, process work sees fears of illness, death and dying as momentary experiences that can be worked with. It also provides tools to work psychologically with illness and the moment of physical death.

In the introduction, I mentioned a time when I was overcome with fear about the changes in my life and my physical health. At that time, my life was undergoing the most rapid change I had experienced since adolescence. For many years I had directed a counseling center in a small town. Suddenly, the clinic lost government funding, and I was thrust not only into financial crisis, but also into an identity crisis, since my central professional focus had been on the clinic. Meanwhile, my wife and I had separated after a long marriage. Just before the clinic failed, I had also bought a new house, and suddenly feared that I would not be able to meet the mortgage payments. My anxiety level escalated.

One week after the clinic lost funding, I dreamed that a friend's father, whom I had never met in ordinary life, came to me. He told me not to worry about money, just to be happy.

In reality, losing one's source of livelihood is like a near-death experience. Similar to a near-death experience, the terror of this event may show the way to something deeper that is to happen. The dream pointed out that I should stay happy and learn to develop the happiness that comes from living in a detached way. When I told my friend about the dream, he said that his father had lived just the way I dreamed about him—he was never overly concerned with making money, and always emphasized being happy. My anxiety was trying in part to help me detach from my fears about the financial world and to live in a more spiritual way.

Next, my anxiety began to manifest as fear about physical symptoms. I became panicky in regard to my health, and went through periods when I was afraid that even the most normal symptoms meant something serious. This was the point at which Mindell said, with a twinkle in his eye, that I was very close to death, but not physical death. The death was of my personal history and my old identity. The married family man, with a small town psychology practice, busy with old psychological complexes, was reaching his end. This Zen-like encounter with Mindell led me to several years of working on the death of my identity. Fritz Perls, the founder of Gestalt Therapy, used to say that dying and being reborn is not easy. When I first came across this concept in my twenties, I had no idea what Perls was talking about. Only in my early forties, going through this upheaval in my identity, did I realize what he meant. Process work has several central concepts that can provide help for people working with issues around illness, death and dying.

Death as an Ally

We have seen in Zen and shamanism that death can remind us to live more fully. Process work also has this concept.

From the process-oriented perspective, fears and fantasies in the area of illness and dying are often seen as coming from our deeper self, the Big You, reminding us of our true path in life. In a modern world where it is easy to be caught up in the mundane details of materialism, death is a reminder that this game is for real. In *The Shaman's Body*, Mindell says that while most people are running away from thoughts of death, the process worker, like the shaman, "...immerses himself in it [death] in order to live more fully."[49]

Mindell goes on to say that

> The Shaman in you lives daily with the sense of death, while the rest of you fights the depressing thought that life will soon be over. I think it is as the shamans say: "Only the sense of imminent death shakes you loose from your momentary attachments and fears, from your interest in the programs you have set up. And so the sorcerer welcomes death as the end to a lifestyle that has long since run out of steam. The shaman finds transformation and ecstasy—not tragedy or failure in death."[50]

This attitude explains how Mindell could laugh and have a twinkle in his eye when I approached him with my terrors of death. He spoke from the Shaman in him, to the Shaman in me, saying that it was my little you, my lifestyle, that needed to change. The programs that I was trying to free myself from were dying. My ordinary personality was frightened; it knew it was running out of time as the director of my life, but it didn't want to be finished. The Big You, which is connected to universal sources outside ordinary life, knew that the little you had to transform for the sake of my personal development.

We often assume that our attachments are to literal outside things such as a job, a spouse, or material things. Mindell helped me wake me up to my attachments to old patterns that did not emphasize happiness—instead, they emphasized suffering, or at best feeling okay. Like the Buddhist masters, he helped me wake up to the dreamlike nature of the patterns I was stuck in. He helped me embrace the death that was coming, and to take death's side in terms of transformation. This attitude was very different than attitudes I had seen modeled in my family and the community. When I was young, people around me reacted to symptoms by becoming terrified and running to doctors, who were not able to address the psychological aspects of their fear surrounding illness and dying.

When we think of death as an ally, it is important to note that awareness of our death is different than being paralyzed or terrorized by death. Being afraid of death may be a beginning step in developing a relationship in which death can serve as an ally. The fear of death is a bit like uncooked bread dough. Raw dough is sticky and not very nourishing, but if we cook it properly, it transforms into a good source of nutrition. Similarly, if we work with our fear of death, it can be transformed into helpful awareness of our death. Don Juan, the shaman in Casteneda's books, says that the shaman carries an awareness of death on their left shoulder.[51] In other words, if we carry an awareness of death, we get down to business and do what is important in life.

Casteneda learns a valuable lesson from Don Juan about the difference between having death as an ally, and becoming paralyzed by death. Casteneda continues to tell Don Juan that he is totally freaked out about death. He says his connection is not helping him; that awareness of death is not an ally, but instead is depressing him. Don Juan tells him that this is because he is obsessed with death, and the way to break this obsession is to stalk himself. Don Juan talks about how death can give people a jolt to get on with their lives, and get on to their true path in life. Since meditating on death doesn't seem to be having this effect for Casteneda, Don Juan comes up with another approach. He recommends poetry.

Poetry, art, drama, dance, music, and social action are some of the creative outlets utilized for centuries by shamans and now by process workers[52] to move beyond the central fears and obsessions of being alive and facing one's inevitable death. The shaman and the process worker know that creativity offers a way to connect people to their own essence, to a place free of anxieties, problems, and complexes. Don Juan and process work both recommend working on deep issues by dropping into one's creativity and expressing the creative essence of what causes panic or anxiety.

As a therapist, I often see people who say that they really wanted to do certain things in life, but that it is now too late for them. Here is an example: Fred came to therapy because he suffered from depression surrounding his job. A professional in his sixties, Fred found his job to be boring much of the time, and needed the security of the money and benefits to satisfy his own sense of safety and desire to care for his family. Fred's relationship partner also found him boring much of the time. Fred complained of feeling dead. As he explored this sense of deadness, he began to discover the importance of being creative in his life. Gradually, he brought this creativity into his home life, his work, and his relationship, and his sense of deadness began to lessen. Fred said that he had always wanted to be a musician, but felt that it was too late. Now, in his sixties, he reconnected with that part of him which was an expressive artist. Fred's sense of deadness can be seen as a sign that his ally was after a change, a personal development, for Fred.

Many people who have lived with cancer speak about it as an ally. I recently bumped into a woman who had been a client years ago. She told me about all the changes she had made since she had left therapy, including changing her relationship, career, lifestyle, and moving to a new city. She noted that it had taken cancer to jolt her into making these positive changes. Even cancer, the disease most feared by many people, helps some people take a leap into their consciousness and their lives. While I always hope that people can make the changes they need without terrifying experiences such as cancer, many people say they couldn't move without such a total shaking up.

Let's look at a related example. A woman once called me in a panic. She said that she was afraid to go to therapy because any therapist would think that she was crazy, but that she had heard I was open to experiences such as the one she was having. She was a professional woman leading an ordinary life, with one exception: she had the irrational experience that a large cat, like a cougar, was chasing her. She dreamt about it at night and felt it after her during the day. While she didn't see it, she felt that this cougar was stalking her.

I didn't think she was crazy at all, which was the first part of her healing. Feeling that something is wrong with our experience prevents us from finding out what might be useful about it. When we began working together, I asked her to do some role-playing with her experience of the cougar. We went back and forth: first I played the cougar, and then she did. When the woman was playing the cougar, she felt tremendous power. As she role-played, she discovered that the cougar wanted her to stop being so mainstream and to start pursuing her spiritual life. This was such a clear message that she followed it. As she had more spirituality in her life, her feeling of being stalked disappeared. This is an example of death, in the form of her cougar ally, telling her to pay attention to her spiritual life. Shamanism, Tibetan Buddhism, Zen, mystical forms of Christianity and Judaism, Taoism, Islam, and other religions all have a similar central teaching—that death is here to remind us of our essential nature which is spiritual and connected to something eternal.

Death, serving as an ally, can remind us to pay attention to what is truly important, to whom we really are. If we are to be closer to our real selves, much of our personal baggage and history need to die. Here's an example. Lucille had worked in the same profession for over twenty years; a medical professional, she was very dedicated to her clients, as well as to her family. Lucille had come from a difficult family background. The messages that she carried from this background were that she wasn't worthy of the good things in life, especially kindness, love, and time and attention for herself.

Lucille originally came to me because she had panicked and simply could not return to her office one day. This event was just the beginning of a long transformation. Several months later Lucille was diagnosed with a serious illness and given little chance of recovery. As she began to work on this, she also began to shed her personal history like a snake sheds old skin. She decided not to return to her old career, at least not in its previous form. She began to fight for what she needed for the first time and asserted herself with the doctors when they didn't treat her well. This woman, who had always been a great advocate for her patients, was finally able to advocate for herself.

As Lucille worked with the patterns from her family of origin, she was able to bring up much of her hurt and anger from the past. She detached from the ongoing pressures of her family members, who expected her to take care of them and live life by their guidelines. She became more assertive at home with her own family, and they began to treat her differently. She let herself do what she needed to heal herself. This approach, along with going through the medical procedures, had a very positive effect. She has so far survived an illness that no medical professional believed she could actually survive.

Here is yet another example. Sherry came in to therapy upset. She had discovered a significant lump in her breast and was scheduled to see a specialist. In therapy, Sherry worked on the qualities and meaning of the lump. She described it as firm, and noted that this was very different from her ordinary personality, which was totally adaptable and malleable, especially to the wants of her husband. As a result of the lump, Sherry began to pay attention to where she wanted to be really solid and take a stand. She discovered that she wanted to change part of her career life but felt that she couldn't because it would hurt the family too much. She said that she would have to become cold to her husband's needs in order to make the change. I encouraged her just to think about making the change, and she felt so energized by the idea that she decided to go ahead and change despite her fears. To her surprise, her husband was concerned about her health and happiness and supported the career change, saying that he would actually get more of what he needed in life if he had his wife back as a happy person.

At this point, an amazing event occurred. Sherry went to see the breast specialist. The lump, which had stayed steady through the several months it took her to finish medical tests and visit various doctors, had totally disappeared. Death didn't want her physical body, but it did want her to pay attention to the changes she needed in life. It demanded that she drop her personal history, which had taught her that a role of a woman was to be soft, giving, and self-obliterating. I have seen similar situations regularly, when a woman with a breast lump experiences a need to become both more assertive and more self-nurturing.

It is common for people who go through such large transformations to change their names. One way to look at this is that they are so far from their old identity that the old name no longer fits. In some ways, people who have made such transformations have died while still alive. A name change might indicate that their personal history as the man or woman with a specific past and patterns is gone. The new person, with a new name, is able to live freely. In Buddhist terms, they have reached a stage of enlightenment; in other words, they have become an eagle, flying freely.

Such transformations may happen gradually; often they are accelerated by the fear of death that suddenly stalks a person, be it a scare from an illness, a loss in career or relationship, or all of these at once.

Fears of Death and Illness as Personal Power

Having gone through times of anxiety and panic myself, I greatly sympathize with the desire that people have to get rid of these feelings. Many of my clients go to see their physicians as a first step to deal with anxiety. We often want to take enough medicine to stop feeling any of these scary feelings. If people ask my advice on medication, I usually recommend that they first try working on their feelings to see what happens, if, of course, they can cope with the level of anxiety that they are experiencing. I make this recommendation because I have so often seen that behind the panic is tremendous energy and power trying to come through.

One of the most dramatic examples of emerging power that I have seen was in a woman who had severe panic attacks. Her attacks were so overwhelming that she sometimes fell to the sidewalk on the way to work, paralyzed with utter terror. She was desperate. Medication had not helped her. She felt absolutely terrified of dying.

As she began to work on her fear and panic, it turned out that she had large issues that she wanted to confront but felt powerless to do so. During a hard time when she couldn't cope, she had given up one of her children. Now she wanted to fight for this child. Her relationship with her partner was full of conflict, and she had unresolved issues with both her mother and father. I encouraged her to try and use her whole self to go ahead and confront all of her issues head on, at one time. She looked at me like I was totally crazy; she was so paralyzed with fear she couldn't even get to work many mornings, and I was suggesting that she tackle all these overwhelming problems in one fell swoop. She was so desperate that she tried the recommendation. Over a three-week period, she began to clean up all the messy areas in her life. A most astonishing thing happened—she began to feel moments of peace and calm. Over the next few months, as she kept moving forward in her life, the panic decreased. The few times her panic attacks recurred, we worked further on where she had gotten stuck. After a few more months, she was completely free of panic. At one point, she noted that while she said that the personal work was extremely difficult and took everything she had, difficult was different and better than panic.

Here is a story from my personal life that illustrates the potential energy available in panic. While out to dinner with friends, someone made a casual comment about their health, which sent me into a real panic. I was awake all night and still felt panicky in the morning. At that point, I decided to meditate on my panic and experiment with being open to it rather than against it. I addressed the panic as my ally and asked it what it wanted from me. The surprising answer was that it wanted me to organize a town meeting on an environmental issue that had polarized the town where I lived. I told my ally that this task was beyond my capabilities, but that I would try anyway. Immediately I felt a great relief, and the meeting that I eventually helped bring about was a positive experience for myself and for so many people in the town.

At other times, my ally has asked me to travel and do conflict resolution work in foreign countries, to write articles and books, to call town meetings on racism, and to change my relationships. As we have developed a more ongoing relationship, my anxiety has decreased. The key in reducing anxiety has not been to do everything I think the ally is asking of me. Instead, it has been to develop a relationship to a part of myself I usually don't identify with.

At this point, you might ask, "Who is the ally?" The ally is a spokesperson for the Big You, the part of yourself connected with the universe. The ally is connected with your deepest purpose, with your dreams and their source. Messages from the ally come from the free and eternal part of yourself; to this part, death is of no real worry.

I have had so many personal experiences of the potential energy in panic, and seen so many clients who have had similar relief when they work with anxieties health and death, that I have grown convinced of the value of working psychologically with such fear. Of course, if a person doesn't have the therapeutic or personal support to work on these issues, medication can be a valuable tool. Also, some people just want medication, or both medication and therapy. If a person does have the appropriate support, there is much potential gain from working through symptoms of anxiety, without medication.

Death as an Ongoing Experience

Process work involves a constant interaction with our momentary deaths. Every time we are willing to leave our fixed identity to risk entering an unfamiliar area, we experience a mini-death of the primary identity. Every time we think that we cannot do, think, feel, or express a certain thing, and then we risk doing it anyway, we risk the death of the Little You for the Big You. The Big You encompasses all parts of a person, including not only the fixed identity but also the growing, emerging parts of the self.

Process work talks about these daily mini-deaths in terms of the *edge*. The edge is where a person feels that they are at the limits of their identity. The edge separates the parts of ourselves that we know and identify with from parts that we don't consider to be part of ourselves. At the edge, where the emerging self comes into being, dreams and symptoms appear. We have seen how this occurs with panic and cancer, which may indicate a person's direction of growth and provide a way of connecting with the Big You.

There are many ways to get to the Big You. One is to die physically. Very close to death, everyone seems to get to this non-dualistic, all-encompassing level. People who have clinically died and been revived often describe the immediate after-death experience as a non-dualistic space of pure experience.[53] I cover these experiences in great detail in Chapter XII on near death experiences. Another way to connect with the Big You is through a near-death experience. Many people report that this puts them in contact with something deep and essential that transforms their experience and life direction.

One conscious way to get in touch with the Big You, which lies beyond our personal edges and the daily identity of the little you, is through *sentient work*. Sentient work is one method of getting to this deep feeling level and picking up subtle processes before they become manifest. There are several ways to do sentient work. One simple method is to sit and meditate. After achieving a quiet state, notice how you identify yourself—you might describe yourself as stressed out, happy, a teacher, a student, etc. After identifying yourself, let your mind become clouded and unknowing, almost foggy. When you have reached this state, ask the universe what it wants of you. Listen and remember what you hear. This simple approach opens the mind to input from a source that we don't generally notice or consider.

Another method of doing sentient work is through flirting with the environment. To flirt with the environment, start by closing your eyes and letting your mind become cloudy. Then, open your eyes and notice whatever first catches your attention. This may surprise you—pay attention to what actually caught your attention, rather than to what you expected to notice. It may be a color, a sound, a person, a smell, or something else in the environment. As you focus on the thing that caught your attention, try this experiment: imagine yourself becoming the thing that attracted you. If you saw a light fixture on the ceiling, see if you can imagine being this light fixture.[54] Once you can imagine yourself as this object, look back at your ordinary self through its eyes. From this new perspective, do you have any advice for yourself, or a message? Let the Big You come through, the part that is big enough to embrace both your normal identity and whatever you flirted with as parts of yourself. You may want to express your wholeness in art, poetry, music, drama, dance, or some other creative form; the sentient parts of us express themselves best through creative means.

Here is one more method of sentient work to try; it is a useful way to learn about things that disturb you. To begin, focus for a moment on something that disturbs you. It might be a relationship problem or a physical symptom. Identify what the experience is like. For example, if it is a headache, it may be a sharp pain, or a pounding. Gradually keep going into the experience until you reach deeper and deeper levels. If you go into the essence of sharpness, beneath it you might fight pressure; beneath the pressure, you may find pulsation. Beneath the pulsation, you might find something like the living beat of the earth. This may be so far down at the bottom that nothing else comes up. When nothing else comes up, you have reached the sentient level. Now, give some kind of creative expression to the sentient experience you arrives at.

In the various spiritual approaches we have addressed thus far, we have seen that the core ideas are very similar.[55] While each approach focuses on the level of universal connection and enduring life, each also brings a special area of focus. In Zen, there is more emphasis on the here and now. Tibetan Buddhism focuses on life and death and the states of transition after death. Shamanism emphasizes using death as an ally in this life, in preparation for one's death. Process work brings a spiritual approach to working with illness, dying, and anxieties about both. Because it works with the whole person and is open to spiritual experiences, process work is a spiritual approach both theoretically and practically. We have seen that working on the dreamlike nature of anxieties often lessens them, as in the case of the woman who felt a cougar stalking her.

Death and Nighttime Dreams

Another way to contact the Big You is through focusing on what one dreams at night. Process work approaches night-time dreams just like daytime anxieties and fantasies, unfolding the message that first appears in the dream. We can often see the evolution of the spiritual process as it progresses throughout a series of dreams. For example, at one point when I was quite anxious about my symptoms, I dreamed that I was walking in a graveyard talking with my dead relatives about what was happening on the other side.

This dream explores my own mini-death. In the dream, I am in an active conversation with those who have already died. As I was beginning to get to the other side of this stage, of working through anxiety, I dreamt that a young boy was wandering around the city. He seemed very lost and scared. When he came up to me, I told him that he must find someone who was a Taoist, who was both a dead person and fully alive. I told him I was such a person.

I saw this dream as a turning point. I was beginning to detach from my worries, and became more helpful to others suffering from anxieties. I was also ready to be helpful to the little boy part of myself who had been so scared by those around him.

I was happy to read later in his book *Taoism, the Road to Immortality*, by John Blofeld, that he writes of something like this dream as the path of the Taoist. He says, "The True man lives in heaven above while remaining on the earth below. He has "left" the world and yet remains within it."[56]

As the series of dreams continued, I dreamt that I had moved beyond my early patterning and was no longer part of the genetic patterning around illnesses that affected my family. I personally believe that freeing oneself from personal history may have such a deep impact on one's physical body that a person may become free from deep genetic patterning. This is an area that will definitely require more research in the future.

Freeing myself from early patterning was definitely a death of some sort. In this particular case, being a dead man meant that I had more detachment from previous patterns on the physical, psychological, relationship, worldly, and spiritual levels.

Parts that are Dying, Parts that are Being Born

On levels from the cellular to the personality, parts of ourselves are always dying, while others are being reborn. Identifying which part is living, which part is dying, and which part is being born can be most helpful as we move through transitions in life. Without training, it is difficult to have an overview about what parts are coming into being as others are passing away. Sometimes the confusion about what is happening is so great that it can become life threatening. We can see this clearly when people become suicidal. Often, when a personality part needs to die, people become confused and think that the physical body itself needs to die. One effective means of suicide prevention is to help people sort out what parts need to pass away.

Let's look at the example of Doug, a teenager who was determined to kill himself. As he explored his desire to die, it became clear that he was desperate for any way out of the social pressures of being a teenager. He was struggling to conform, while his true nature was not at all traditional. In therapy, he was able to express the ways in which he did not conform to the environment. He was deeply concerned about the fate of the old growth forests. In an area where many people worked in the timber industry, this was a frightening view for a young person to hold. As Doug was able to express his position, he began to speak up in school and joined a group of environmentalists. When his true identity was able to express itself, suicide stopped being an issue.

Here is another example of how suicide is not necessarily about a desire to kill one's whole self. Jane was one of the most suicidal people I had ever met. She had been on many different medications, but still felt that she would kill herself. For many sessions, we both had a difficult time. She declared repeatedly that I was wasting my time. I spoke into the air, about her Zen-like nature, about the spirit I felt in her presence. I attempted to work with her on relationship issues with her friends, her family of origin, her education and career, but she was disinterested in all of these areas. The only time she seemed interested was when I talked about shamanism, spirituality, and reincarnation.

Because Jane already seemed detached from her personal history, I began to think that she might be on a path of detachment, which was unusual for someone so young.

Following her positive feedback in this area, I suggested that she let go of her history and stop focusing on herself as the child of a particular family. Over time, a remarkable change occurred in Jane. She grew interested in deep questions about the meaning of life and even began to find a sense of meaning. At one point, she decided it was time to find new friends, since her current friends were too depressed - much like her old identity. Jane became increasingly free to be herself. She started speaking up, sharing her ideas, and left her old suicidal identity by the wayside. In this example, we see that Jane felt suicidal when what needed to change was her sense of identity based on her personal history. She was ready to kill that part and move on to identifying with her fascination in life and in the mysteries of life. Connecting with this level was a source of great energy and inspiration.

Comatose experiences, like suicidal ideation and near death experiences, sometimes offer a new direction in life, if we can find and live the messages they bring. Phil was a young man who fell into a coma due to a severe head injury received in an auto accident. As I worked with him in his comatose state, I reminded him that he was free to come out of the coma and be whoever he wanted to be. Phil eventually emerged from his coma. Upon awakening, he had left behind the part of him that didn't take life seriously. As he recovered, many friendships fell by the wayside, since the old Phil, who had died, was a wild party animal. The new Phil had an irrevocable sense of direction and purpose in life, and he didn't fit in at all with his previous crowd. Many people who come out of coma and recover fully say that they are happier with the new part of their personality that emerged after coma.[57]

Summary

Process work embraces many of the ideas we have seen in other spiritual traditions in relations to how to work with illness and death anxieties. Process work also makes a unique contribution with its methods of working with these anxieties in the here and now.

This chapter focused on two main aspects of process work with fears of death. We saw that death can serve as an ally that helps us wake up to our whole self. We also learned how to discover death as an ally both by working on our personal edges and mini-deaths, and by exploring the sentient level of awareness. The second part of this chapter showed that we could work with death in every moment by discovering and working with the parts of ourselves trying to die and the other parts trying to be reborn.

Exercises

The following four exercises on sentient work are based on exercises developed and taught by Arnold and Amy Mindell in their workshops on sentient work. I am thankful to them for these exercises, which I utilize repeatedly when working with clients and myself.

EXERCISE: Introductory Sentient Work

1. Sit quietly and take a few breaths. Think for a moment about your purpose in life, and an area where you are struggling to live out that purpose.
2. Close your eyes and let your mind become cloudy and unknowing. When your mind is empty, slowly open your eyes and notice whatever first catches your attention.

3. Shape-shift into the thing that caught your attention. For example, if you saw a picture of a river on the wall, become the river.
4. Now imagine that you could look back at yourself through the eyes of the river (or whatever caught your attention.). What does the river see when it looks at you?
5. Next, see if you can look at yourself and the river from the perspective of the Big You, which sees both the river and you as part of the same whole. Take this as a momentary picture of the deeper you that is trying to be present.
6. Imagine that you are this whole self. As your whole self, remember your original struggle about your purpose in life. Is there any way in which having access to your whole self might help with your struggles in this area?

EXERCISE: Symptoms Work and Sentient Work

1. Chose a difficult symptom, present or past, and preferably one you can feel.

EXERCISE: Dreamland

1. Focus on the symptom and feel all the details of it.
2. Now focus not on the effect of the symptom, but on the initial energy. For example, with a headache, focus on the sharpness of it, not on the tiredness it produces.
3. Express the original energy of the symptom in movement, and try to catch an image that goes with this movement. Try to find out what this energy is expressing or doing.

4. Make a note about the root, the sentient essence of your experience in steps 2-4 above.
5. If that essence had a whole world, what would it be like? What would the time and space of that essence's world be like?
6. Climb into the world of the symptom and explore it. Let it unfold creatively and see what kinds of images or poetry start to unfold. Maybe music or movement also want to happen.
7. Consider how this experience might influence your daily life. Is there any way this experience has already appeared in your life?
8. Re-feel the essence of the symptom. From that place, can you see what your ordinary self might need? From that place, do you have specific advice about how to care for your body?

EXERCISE: Momentary Living and Dying

This exercise is designed to work directly on anxieties about death, and is best done with a friend.

1. Describe who you are now in the moment.
2. What are you most anxious about dying from? A disease, an accident?
3. Lie down and imagine that you are dying of whatever causes your worst anxiety about death.
4. In your imagination, watch yourself die. As you keep watching, notice the transformation. What becomes of you after you die? Are you a part of the earth? Do you become part of nature, or a ghost, spirit, or star? Do you quickly reincarnate?

5. Express whatever you become after death creatively in poetry, dance, art, movement, or song.
6. Imagine that this is the new you. What part of yourself died, and what has been born or reborn?
7. Talk about how you might need to make these changes in your life? Are you already making them somehow?

| CHAPTER 7 |

Taoism

Taoism and Life

In this chapter, we will look at the aspects of Taoism that I have found most helpful in working with anxieties about life and death. A wonderful source on Taoism, and one that directly addresses anxiety, is John Blofeld's *Taoism, The Road to Immortality*. Blofeld says that a deep sense of peace about life and death naturally emerges from Taoism's central focus on following nature. In his words,

> A dedicated Taoist is one who seeks to live as closely in accord as possible with nature...to go along with nature effortlessly, as does a fish or a master artisan, is to swim with the current, to let one's knife slip along the grain. When nature is taken as a guide, a friend, living becomes almost effortless, tranquil, joyous, even. Care departs; serenity takes over.[58]

In each moment, the Taoist asks how she can best follow nature. This provides an answer to the fear of living and dying. Blofeld says, "Free from greed, free from strain, a stranger to anxiety and fear, the sage takes whatever action may be needed, stopping the very moment his objective is attained, and far from congratulating himself on it success, puts it out of his mind as soon as it is done."[59] He goes on to say that this helped the masters keep strong minds and bodies, often until reaching an advanced age, because the lack of stress and anxiety brought about so little wear and tear on their beings.[60]

The implications of being devoted to following nature are clear. If the direction is life, the Taoist embraces that, and if the direction is death, then one embraces that. There is no sense of anxiety with either possibility. Blofeld says it clearly when he says, "For the present, the adept seeks to live in harmony with nature, enjoying happiness in the here and now, serenely indifferent to what may follow since, to one lives wisely, everything happens for the best, whether death comes sooner or later."[61] Along with this here and now living is the cultivation of the immortal, spiritual body. In this is great liberation, since the liberated consciousness is reunited with the entire universe. As Blofeld says, "Could there ever, ever be a more glorious endeavor?"[62] The many spiritual practices of Taoism are designed to help the Taoist cultivate both living freely in the here and now and to reach eternal freedom and liberation.

Like Zen Buddhism, Taoism is concerned with developing inner freedom. The Taoist master Ni Hua-Ching says that "Taoist internal alchemy is a process for actualizing the development of the inner being from a mechanical pattern of life to a life of absolute freedom."[63]

In Taoism, the central purpose of life is developing this absolute freedom. Many Taoist methods focus on longevity, not for the sake of simply adding years to a life, but for the sake of having more time to develop and gain this sense of freedom. The Taoists view life and death as parts of a continuous process. As Ni-Hua Ching says, "The cycle of incarnation occurs through the pattern of life and death. Life does not mean a start. Death does not mean an end. People who consider a human life from birth to death as the whole life are misled. ... Life itself is a continual process of transformation and evolution."[64]

Taoism and Reincarnation

Taoism presents a fascinating and tangible picture of how reincarnation occurs. Chang Tzu sums up the beliefs of Taoism when he says, "Life is the companion of death: death is the beginning of life." He goes on to say," Some day there will be a great awakening when we shall know that all this is a dream."[65] Master Ni-Hua Ching says that birth and death cycles occur every 120 years. We spend 120 years on earth; it may take a number of lifetimes to reach 120 years in the life cycle. Then we spend 120 years in what the Taoists call the shadow world, which is an invisible realm. At that point, we return to a series of lifetimes until we again reach 120 years. In his theory, people usually reincarnate according to kinship, meaning that we go back to the same family lineage. He says that members of the same family often come back to their children and grandchildren. This is similar to the Kabbalists who talk of us going back to our families and our relationships again and again. He also postulates a law of passion in reincarnation, which says that if you strongly love or hate someone, it is likely you will return as their child. Finally, he notes that attachment to community or nation will partially determine where you reincarnate. He cautions people not to hate others too much, since one can be reborn into the enemy's family and thus have a very hard time.[66]

In Taoism, the purpose of life is to be true to your own center of being. What feeds the center of being is living with virtue in life, which means to be positive, constructive, and creative. How one lives life on earth will greatly influence one's experiences in the 120 years on the shadow side. This concept has certain similarities to the Tibetan Buddhist ideas of the Bardo states in the afterlife, in that what a person experiences in the afterlife is not random and uncontrollable. Afterlife experiences are shaped by what one did in life; also, one's ability to face these experiences in the afterlife is determined by the skills and virtues one has developed while living.

In Taoism, as in Buddhism, it is possible to step off the wheel of reincarnation. The Taoists believe that the *shien*, or the Immortals, have stepped off the wheel. Like the Buddhist Boddhisatva, the Immortals are free to reincarnate wherever they like, and only if they like. Blofeld says of the immortals and death: "Death, when it comes, will be for him no more than the casting off of a worn out robe. He has won to eternal life and is ready to plunge back into the limitless ocean of pure being."[67] Once in this realm, the immortal is free to travel to any realm.

While living, the Taoists cultivate a sense of virtue that builds one's light. The goal is to become one's whole self, to let one's true nature shine forth. By devoting oneself to one's true nature, one becomes dedicated to following the eternal path, which is called the Tao.

Taoism, Reincarnation, and Anxieties about Death

Taoism may help alleviate anxiety about death by providing a tangible view of reincarnation. When we think about those who have died, or about our own death, much of our sadness is often related to losing contact with loved ones. From a Taoist point of view, we are with each other again and again, so we don't lose contact with those we love forever. In addition, Taoism believes that we do not die permanently when we leave life. Instead, we enter the shadow realms for a time before we return to the manifestation realms. The Taoist view, which sees death and life as fluid states within a larger cycle, helps many people feel more peaceful about the inevitability of death.

Let's look at an example. Pat had recently lost her father. She felt robbed of his presence and felt that their relationship had stopped abruptly with his death. When I suggested that death didn't have to be the end of a relationship, she became quite interested. She worked in therapy on the feelings she hadn't been able to express directly in her relationship with her father. As she worked through her feelings, she began to have strong dreams about her father. For the first time since childhood, she became convinced that he really loved her. She felt his loving presence in a way she hadn't known for years. Her experience of him and their relationship changed completely.

This example brings up many interesting questions. What is life when Pat's father was physically alive but emotionally distant? What is death, in which Pat feels his loving presence more than ever? Which is life and which is death? As we heard earlier from the Zen master, it is very difficult to answer this question.

Cultivating One's Eternal Nature

Taoism may also help with anxieties about dying by offering methods to cultivate one's eternal nature. These methods include inner work and meditation along with external work and virtuous living. Similar to Zen Buddhism, cultivation of the Tao generally involves losing the ego. Master Ni Hua-Ching summarizes twenty-one steps towards cultivating the Tao.[68]

Several of his steps are particularly useful in moving beyond anxieties about living and dying. The first principle is to dissolve the ego and unite with the eternal. We have seen a similar concept at the core of many spiritual teachings, which all talk about going beyond the limited self into the greater self. Another useful principal concerns living simply. The Taoists are minimalists in terms of the physical and material world; they live simply in order to nurture the spiritual parts of life. They are dedicated to serving others, which is a key part of move beyond the ego. Finally, in following nature, they take it easy, not overindulging or feeling stressed or enslaved by old habits; this helps cultivate a deep sense of freedom, which is by its nature not conducive to anxiety.

Summary

Taoism teaches both meditation techniques and principles to live by. If one believes that these methods will help cultivate inner light and the eternal nature this reflects, then Taoism can help bring peace of mind and a sense of connection to the eternal. Taoism postulates that transcending the wheel of life and death is not just a matter of luck; those who wish to live in a certain way can actively advance themselves on this path.

EXERCISE: Living as a Taoist

1. Take a journal and go to a beautiful place in nature.
2. Take time to meditate on this beauty, to let it in.

3. Ask yourself how you could simplify your life to be more attuned to nature, to follow her, and to have time to cultivate more of your spiritual life.
4. Make some notes of what comes through you as you meditate.

| CHAPTER 8 |

Core Approches to Life and Death

This chapter covers five basic approaches towards life and death. People tend to occupy these positions at various times in their lives, and there is not always a linear progression from position one through position five. People also tend to have one of these positions as a core attitude toward life and death.

The Five Core Approaches

People with the "I don't care if I am alive or dead attitude" live life on automatic pilot. Disconnected from life and death, these people wait and long for physical death. People with the second attitude, which I call "tied to the wheel," are more alive and slightly more connected with death than people with the first attitude. Their primary life goal is to avoid death and insecurity. People with this attitude frequently experience anxiety about health matters, money, job security, relationship security, and death. Our culture encourages this position through its general denial of death. The third attitude is "becoming detached." People identified with this position have reconnected with the parts of themselves that were previously marginalized. They are working beyond the limits of their personal identities and identifying more with the spiritual sides of themselves. People with this attitude are aware of death, which becomes an ally rather than a terrifying foe. People with the fourth attitude of "living fully," know that death is a moment of awesome proportions that requires tremendous awareness. These people are living so fully that death is just one more moment to be experienced. At this stage, people have gone past experiencing the polar opposites of living and dying and can face death with a deep acceptance of all feelings and experiences present. Life has been lived to such an extent that people, while they may not want to die, can die with few regrets.

The fifth attitude is "facing death with equanimity." This part of ourselves is close to enlightenment. People at this stage neither long for nor fear death. They are committed to living fully right until the moment of death. For them, death and life are part of a much bigger circle, and they are connected to both the personal and transpersonal parts of themselves. They are connected to their whole selves and to the whole of life, and to the dead.

In previous chapters, we have been talking about collective approaches to living and dying. In addition to these larger collective forces, each individual develops a unique attitude towards life and death. Often these individual approaches are formed largely in our family of origin. Some families fear dying and focus a great deal on not getting ill; these families may worry about health and make frequent trips to medical doctors. Other families, while not particularly focused on dying, strongly emphasize being safe, secure, and avoiding risks. In some families, there is a sense of balance and some detachment from death, so that family members don't avoid the topic of death, nor do they feel obsessed with it. Some families use death as an ally to encourage living fully and freely. In some cases, families live so fully and do so much personal growth that they face death with freedom and acceptance.

These various attitudes towards life and death influence how we live on a daily basis. Let's take a look more now at the details of how they can be categorized, and how they influence life.

Life Isn't Worth Living

Many people have a core attitude that life isn't really worth living; that it doesn't matter if one is alive or dead. These people go through life on automatic pilot, marking time until the end. Life can involve a great deal of suffering. In some families, the levels of suffering seem so great that people seem to have given up being interested in life. Death becomes the only relief from the suffering and grind of life. Sometimes in families with this kind of depression in the background, there is a great deal of illness and people dying at a young age. In families where there is a great deal of serious illness, we often find some sort of multigenerational abuse in the background, or other sources of depression or trauma. People in such families are often addicted to substances such as alcohol as an attempt to numb the pain of existence. We may find suicide attempts, or a high number of accidents. The early deaths are often tied to specific kinds of behavior that are directly suicidal, or like in the case of alcohol or cigarettes, may be slower ways to kill oneself. This should not be taken to say that people choose to die, or are responsible for whether they live or die. This is much more causal than I believe. I am talking here about tendencies, which are present in all of us all the time, and influence us in constant ways that may affect the chances of us living or dying. For example, notice the way you drive on a day when you are extremely upset and down. Then notice how you drive when you are feeling really good and thinking about all the people you love and who love you. You might be extra careful on those days, taking better care of yourself. Maybe you are sure to pull off and rest when tired. On another day when you are angry and down, maybe you speed more, take the curves a bit faster, don't really watch with as much awareness as to what is going on around you. The attitudes in the background influence most of our daily decisions. What we eat, our addictions, how we take care of ourselves in our work, our relationships, our creativity, all are influenced by this core attitude.

In families with a high degree of trauma in the background, making decisions that may hasten death may actually seem like a good idea, since life is so painful that it isn't really a positive option. While people don't choose death, they may make conscious or unconscious decisions to hasten death. Saying people choose death makes it sounds like a conscious process, but most people are unconscious about the self-destructive aspects of many parts of their behavior. Once people become aware of self-destructive behavior, then it can be said they are choosing death. However, people are generally unconscious about their attitudes around life and death, and about the choices they make to hasten death or to live life fully. Freeing oneself from the pervasive attitude that life is not worth living usually requires the assistance of a skilled therapist, spiritual teacher, or both.

Any person who is able to free himself or herself from such a pattern has made a break in a family pattern; from their new perspective, they may be able to help others in the family system break free from what is usually an unconscious family pattern. The depression in the background of such families, if worked with, often transforms into the kind of detachment that helps a person feel free in life.

Here is an example. Larry had come from a terrible background of neglect and abuse. As an adult, his self-destructive behaviors, including his addictions, resulted in his losing his job and his family. He took increasingly dangerous paths to help distract him and ease his pain. Many of his friends pointed out these behaviors and his increasing brushes with death, but he still continued. Yet a part of him was determined to work it out. He worked through layer after layer of the pain. He listened to where I saw his behaviors as self-destructive. He listened to my regular strong but loving confrontations on where he was in denial to many of these behaviors, and where he was killing himself. Slowly things began to change. Larry took two steps forward, one back, and finally began to work with all of his strength to move through his patterns and stop his addictions. While some of the people in treatment programs that Larry skipped out of died, Larry made it. He succeeded: his family took him back and he got a job. Perhaps most important, he picked up on his spirituality. He became a new person, and his attitude towards life and death changed. At times, he had deep regrets for what he had gone through, and at other times he understood that if he had not brushed so close to death he wouldn't have discovered his unconscious ambivalence around living. He is young still, and if he keeps on this path, he will become the shaman I saw present when he told me his dreams. He left behind his personal history, and became instead, closer to living out his essence.

Being Tied to the Wheel

Another common attitude toward living and dying is to live cautiously. In individuals and families with this attitude, the focus is on staying safe and avoiding risks; the reward of this approach is avoiding death.

We may see this attitude manifesting as worry about the body. In the area of health, people with this attitude may spend a lot of time visiting doctors and taking medical tests, with the goal of determining that they will not die soon or won't have a serious illness.

For example, I once had a client who often began the session by reporting her latest medical test results. She never had anything seriously wrong with her, and the test results were always negative. We began to focus our work on where she really wanted to be in her life and on what would truly make her happy. As she worked on discovering her goals, and on developing the freedom to follow them, she gradually became less concerned with taking medical tests.

This attitude may also appear as an inability to take risks and give up the status quo.

In areas of life such as relationships, work, and spiritual practice, the main emphasis is on stability and security. For example, I have seen many jaws fall open in shock when I suggest that a person leave a job that they hate. Of course, safety and security are important; the point is that safety can become so overly emphasized that people become closed to all other options.

The cautious attitude toward life values longevity. One important question to consider is whether or not this attitude helps to ensure a long life. Does not taking risks, or worrying about illness, lead to living longer? I am not convinced that it does; nor does it necessarily enhance quality of life, since it is difficult to be truly happy if one's main emphasis is safety.

One of the pitfalls of this approach to life is that change and impermanence are central aspects of life. Trying to create a world with no change sets a person up for insecurity and does not prepare them for the inherent changes in life.

Process work theory has often addresses the health benefits in taking personal risks and living at the edge of one's development. For example, a woman's husband once carried her into my office because she had injured her back. Right before the injury, she had had a terrible time with her boss. Her need for security told her to just keep taking it from the boss. However, the stress levels had become so great that she had so much back pain she couldn't go to work. She couldn't even stand up. In a role-play, we had her go over the edge. She told the boss off, but in a way that she imagined she might even keep her job. She also began to kick her legs and have a bit of a fit. Her back pain left immediately, and she was so happy she got up and ran down the stairs.

This example illustrates an important concept. While many people feel that they must not bring out any of their feelings or reactions at work, because they would risk losing a job, keeping such reactions inside may often lead to depression or manifesting physical symptoms. Surprisingly, keeping in all of one's reactions is not actually a safe move in the long run. A safer move would be to find some way to access their feelings and do something with the energy of being so unhappy. For example, I remember a man who got very depressed over work issues. After he was able to express all of his upset feelings in my office, he came up with all kinds of creative ideas for how to change this job scene. While going over the edge may at times risk short term security, it may also lead to deeper solutions that in the long run may be much more secure.

This cautious attitude is like being caught in a revolving door. There is no way out, because another anxiety is always waiting around the corner. During periods of anxiety about my health, I experienced this cycle repeatedly. When a test turned out negative, I would celebrate a moment of freedom, but then another anxiety emerged. This momentary relief is not real freedom. Pursuing relief from health anxieties is like a dog chasing its tail; it is hard to feel healthy in an internal and external system that emphasizes health problems and anxieties. Few people are genuinely happy going to doctors and focusing on their potential for illness; this is a path of great suffering for most people.

This cycle is vicious in another way; when people aren't happy; their unhappiness in life easily translates to the fear that something is physically wrong. For example, I was very unhappy in my late teen years. While I had a great relationship with my first real love, I was unhappy in school and had family problems. While I was very athletic, I was small. Coaches cut me from the teams, no matter how good I was, because I didn't fit the athletic norms. I was also strongly influenced by the political climate. During the Vietnam War protests, I felt pulled between the radical views of my friends and the conservative views of my family. While I was growing up, the extended family was always around, which meant constant arguments between the three generations present. I was suffering from the pressures of being in a competitive school, having my first important relationship, and trying to deal with my sexuality and vulnerability. Now, it's clear that what was really going on for me back then was a typical adolescent identity crisis.

Not knowing how to deal with my shifting identity, I focused instead on my digestive problems. I saw many doctors, who took x-rays and did tests and told me everything was fine. Looking back, it is clear that I was looking for something physical to pin my existential angst on. This approach is common in adults as well as teens. While the real problem might be that a person hates work, or has relationship issues, or is haunted by an abuse history, people often focus on physical symptoms instead of the underlying issue. Focusing on a physical symptom can provide temporary relief, since it provides a name and focus for the deep pain in a person's life. This relief is usually temporary, because the symptom gets better while the underlying feelings stay the same.

There is also a physical component that ties us to this attitude. Certain physical body processes require deep periods of relaxation. If you are always worried, it is hard to experience the kind of relaxation that makes you feel well. For example, when I was so uptight about my health and I couldn't relax, my digestion, which was never great, made me feel unwell, which made me think something was wrong. The cycle can repeat itself like this for years. Another example is how people worry about the effects of stress, which causes more stress, which causes one to feel more symptomatic.

The only way to stop chasing one's tail around health issues is to change one's relationship to life and death. Relaxation techniques can be helpful here, since they remind your body what it is like to feel relaxed and provide temporary relief from stress symptoms. True relaxation requires having the freedom to follow oneself through periods of intensity, and periods of deep relaxation, finding one's own unique way to balance the needs for both. Some people ultimately need to alternate between intensity and relaxation, while others need to integrate the two states, learning how to maintain intense awareness during relaxation, and learning to relax in the midst of intensity.

One of the problems with this attitude is that getting medical reassurance, and feeling temporarily relieved, can be addictive. The temporary relief you find when you aren't sick is like a momentary high. This cycle is addictive in several aspects. First, many people feel out of control because the only time they feel that they are okay is after receiving reassurance from an outside medical source. This is similar to turning to a substance to feel okay about oneself. Second, there can be harmful consequences to being addicted to medical reassurance. Medical visits can be harmful—they often involve stress, lost money and time, and side effects from tests such as x-rays. Being obsessed with one's health can aggravate one's partner; I have seen relationships come to the brink of dissolution because one person obsesses over their health. This is similar to an addiction in that one partner is more focused on their substance abuse, or in this case health, than they are on the relationship.

Another way in which the constant need for medical reassurance resembles addiction is in the area of family patterning. Often this sort of obsession is a shared family trait, and there is pressure to keep doing it, just as some families pressure their members to keep drinking alcohol. Families will often say to a member who is trying to break the habit of going to doctors that they should really have certain things checked by a physician. Since medical addiction is often part of family culture, an individual must either break out of it alone, or the whole family may need to change.

Finally, most addictions give temporary relief, not full satisfaction. One power of addictive drugs is that they provide a taste of what a person is seeking. An addiction to doctors and the medical system is similar because the temporary high of hearing that everything is fine doesn't last. When a person doesn't really feel fine about life, they are stuck in the cycle of returning for that next drink, that next drug, or that next medical visit that leaves them feeling temporarily free, well, and fine.

Other forms of security can be equally as addictive. The security of a salary and benefits from a job that is harmful to oneself can be addictive. People may be addictive to relationships that are secure, even if they are destructive. Many of us choose a known hell rather than risking a potential unknown heaven.

This attitude toward life also carries a great potential. Behind the anxiety and need for security, we often find energy and power. This energy, if freed to become fully creative, can carry a person forward on their life path. The longing for security can sometimes push people to discover what really makes them feel secure in life. True security often has more to do with being one's whole self and fulfilling one's deepest dreams in life than with simply being safe, which can become deadening.

Here is an example. Sam came to see me because he was miserable in his long-term relationship. The one thing he felt he could not do was feel separate from his wife. He had once been a very powerful, independent man, but had become increasingly dependent on his wife. He felt that he couldn't be separate anymore, that it was just too scary and would destroy his family. When Sam was encouraged to experiment with his separateness, he was at first just terrified. However, the more he worked on this, the more excited he got. He remembered this other side of himself. He regained his interests in creativity, art, and other fields. He remembered his love for travel. He took some steps on his own. The more risks he took to do this, the less he resented his relationship, and the more energy he had for his family and partner.

His perceptions of togetherness and separateness began to shift from polar opposites to related states that flowed into each other. Through risking momentary terror and fears of dissolution of his family and perhaps his personality, Sam reconnected with himself, re-energized himself, and reconnected with his family in a way that was sustainable.

Becoming Detached

Another attitude, which generally occurs only after people have begun to work consciously on their attitudes toward living and dying, is something like, "sort of alive, becoming more dead." People with this attitude have become more detached from their personal history and conventional expectations for how they should feel and behave. As people become freer from their own personal history and society's expectations, they are freer to be themselves and live fully. People with this attitude generally experience increasing happiness. While one is developing this more detached attitude, confusion between the detachment of spiritual transformation and body anxiety still occurs. During this phase, people often find that they can pull themselves out of anxiety more quickly. There is more detachment from the physical body, and from the various relationship and life difficulties that fuel anxiety. For people from families that worry about health, it is much easier, at this phase, to create psychological distance from the family and their patterns.

It is interesting to note that during this developmental stage, people's dreams often reflect their growth beyond family patterns and a new identification with a universal self. It is common for people to dream that the earth is their mother, the sky or the sun their father, that they have angels or other protectors with them. They may dream of spiritual teachers, or about communicating with dead relatives or friends who reveal the secrets of life and death. For example, during a phase when I was becoming more detached, I dreamt repeatedly that my parents were the earth, the sun, and the sky. I was developing a new attitude towards life that needed to be parented by spiritual parents. My birth parents gave me a great deal in life, but not this particular attitude.

Creativity often comes to the forefront as people become more detached from personal history. Painting, writing, poetry, music, drama, dance, or other art forms serve to express the true self as it emerges. As people become less preoccupied with their own worries and concerns, they often develop increased energy for social action and other worldly tasks. As we emerge from our own pain and suffering, there is usually a greater feeling of compassion for others. Many people dream of becoming teachers, healers, or world leaders as this new attitude begins to develop.

Relationships also begin to transform at this point. Old patterns, which people thought would last forever, may begin to shift in radical ways. I remember a time when my relationship style, which included expressing lots of anger verbally to my partner, just shifted. I dreamt that it was over, that something new needed to happen, and it did. My partner could not believe at first that I was no longer expressing so much anger verbally, but once the shift occurred, I never went back.

When I tell the people how angry I used to be, they have trouble believing it. While I am not against being angry, how I express my anger in relationships has changed completely. I no longer have a program that anger must be expressed verbally. I have much more freedom around being angry. I can ask myself if expressing anger is going to foster the relationship and lead to something positive. Once I start getting angry, I can avoid going ballistic by reminding myself that I don't want to destroy the relationship. As I said to my partner recently, I can notice the part of myself which would like to lose it and attack the whole relationship, while another part reminds me that this is a bad moment within a great relationship. This kind of awareness and freedom isn't possible without a sense of detachment from personal history.

Many people report similar dramatic changes in their relationships. For example, let's look at the relationship between Shelly and Harry. Shelly had had a painful childhood in which family members sexually abused her. Her intimate and sexual interactions with Harry had always been strained. Although she had worked extensively on her abuse history, nothing changed their relationship. When Shelly and Harry came to therapy, Shelly's dreams seemed to suggest that she was done with her personal history, which she had worked on for so long. In her dreams, Shelly was living in new houses, remodeling, traveling to new worlds. She dreamt that people from her childhood had died. As Shelly experimented with dropping her old identity and letting this old part of her life die, she began to experience breakthroughs with Harry. For example, she reported feeling sexually free for the first time in her life.

As Shelly changed, Harry also had to develop. He sometimes described the old Shelly without appreciating the changes in her that were right in front of his eyes. He also had to support and allow the death and transformation to happen. For example, he had to own the part of himself that enjoyed feeling like the more emotionally capable partner. He also had to work more on his issues from childhood, which had been ignored as the two of them focused on Shelly's difficulties. Over time, their whole relationship system became increasingly focused on living in the here and now rather than in the past or in their previous conceptions of each other.

Living Life Fully

Another development in the attitudes toward life and death is the "living fully" stage. At this stage, a person is increasingly free to follow their own inner guidance in relation to living life. At this point, people tend to feel more detachment from external rules and regulations and are less bound by the conventions of ordinary reality. While people may still choose to follow society's rules, they do so with a sense of understanding about where these rules come from, and are free to choose which ones to follow and which not to follow. People tend to follow their individual dreams more fully, knowing that taking risks is a part of life, and that we all die some day. When people who have reached this stage of life reach their time to die, they tend to die with more good memories and fewer regrets than people who are living with the goal of avoiding death. For many of us, avoiding death is an unconscious attitude. When a person goes to their deathbed with this attitude, both the person and the medical professionals involved often feel that they have failed and that the worst has come.

People who have lived fully may not feel ready to die, but when they review their lives around the time of death, many say that they have lived fully. Sometimes living fully only happens near the end of life, when a person pursues a dream, such as travel or taking a class. Some people say that they loved fully, or made the world a better place.

Part of living fully that we have not discussed thus far is being comfortable with one's inner life. Feeling at home inside oneself not only helps us pursue our outer dreams, but also helps us feel comfortable with altered states of consciousness. If a person hasn't done much spiritual and psychological inner work, the altered states that come up near death can be disturbing and difficult. If people live their inner lives fully, they learn to embrace altered states during meditation, dream work, bodywork, relationship work, spiritual work and creativity.

Learning to feel comfortable with altered states of consciousness is part of the Tibetan Buddhist emphasis on working with death while alive. In *The Tibetan Book of Living and Dying*, Sogyal Rinpoche talks about how advanced masters, who have worked on their psychological and spiritual selves, usually have positive experiences while dying. He notes that people who have not had the opportunity to develop psychologically and spiritually often have experiences that are more difficult. The altered states around death can provide a springboard for rapid personal growth, since they give people access to parts of themselves they didn't know were present. Altered states bring out parts of ourselves that lie beyond our ordinary personalities. If we know these parts during life, meeting them near death is like greeting old friends. If we haven't become familiar with altered states, the images and feelings that come up around dying can be shocking and frightening.

As people become freer to live out their deepest callings and dreams, they often feel a growing sense of happiness and inner peace. For example, Sally, who had always dreamed of being a psychotherapist, had spent her whole career life in the business world. At age sixty, she felt that it was far too late to pursue her dream of becoming a therapist. Ageism often comes in, as a cultural force that tells us it is too late to embrace our dreams. As Sally worked beyond this cultural bias and returned to school, she grew happier and happier.

A special glow of deep happiness is often a sign that people have reached this stage of development. This deep happiness doesn't mean that life is without great difficulties; it just means that on a core level, people know that they are on the right track. Frank is a good example. At age 75, he had a stroke that left him in a coma. Before the coma, he had been a very rational person. After he came out of the coma, he was much more emotional and sensitive to himself and to people around him. Before Frank died, he had made peace in his close relationships in a new way for him, and his death was sudden and painless. As he was able to express his whole self, rather than just the rational side, not only was he able to let go and die, but also his loved ones could let go and celebrate his life.

To live fully, a person must bring forth their whole self. Most of us tend to hold ourselves back and rarely feel free to bring out all of our energy. There are many outlets for full expression of our energy, including athletics, creativity, sexuality, spirituality, and social action. Living fully means working to make room for the parts of ourselves we usually push aside. As we grow up, messages from family and society encourage us to marginalize increasingly more parts of ourselves. We hear: Don't be aggressive, don't cry, girls don't do this, boys don't do that, don't be too sensual.

I remember certain ways that I marginalized parts of myself based on the messages I received. When I was ill as a child, the family pediatrician did not encourage me to trust my body and my deep feelings of connection to my healing process. At that point, I began to lose my intuition about what my body needed in order to heal. In elementary school, the art teacher told me that I had no potential in art and should not take any more classes. At that point, I marginalized my artistic nature. As we try to fit in with society, we push more and more of our powers and parts away. In addition to marginalization of our individual qualities, we all face pressure to conform to mainstream society. In the West, being white, heterosexual, Christian, male, educated, and successful is valued more than being a person of color, gay, lesbian, bisexual or trans-gendered, Jewish or Muslim or Buddhist, less educated, or poor. People who don't fit into the valued categories tend to feel even less desirable.

Living fully requires retrieving and reactivating the parts of ourselves we have pushed aside. If a fifty-year-old person brings back the sensual part they put away at age nineteen, the current sensual self may be different from the youthful one, but it has its own vitality. Reclaiming our anger at forty often requires a different form of expression than we had at age seven, but the essential power of expression remains.

There are many ways to recover lost parts of ourselves. One useful method comes from shamanism. Shamans call retrieving parts of ourselves we have split off *soul retrieval*. Sandra Ingerman, who wrote a book called *Soul Retrieval*, goes into great detail on these matters. She defines soul loss as the effects of trauma, noting that whenever we experience trauma, we react by splitting off a part of our vital essence. Shamanic systems believe that the split-off essence goes into non-ordinary reality where it can be retrieved through the shaman's journey.[69] Ingerman also points out that shamans the world over have associated illness with this loss of soul, of vital energy, and therefore, soul retrieval offers a path of healing that is spiritually based.[70]

When people begin to reclaim lost parts of themselves, their dreams often have themes that reflect this development. For example, a person might dream that they return to the house they grew up in, but then happily discover that the house has many additional beautiful rooms. Dreams like this reflect the process of reconnecting with important pieces of oneself that were once more accessible; in their newly discovered forms, they have the potential to bring much happiness.

Soul retrieval is based on a similar concept. In this world-view, we are born with certain powers that protect us; through acculturation and the trauma of life, we may lose contact with these parts of ourselves, which we will then have to reclaim. In many tribal cultures, these powers are symbolized by a power animal, and people cultivate a relationship with their power animals throughout a lifetime. Celebrating one's power animal happens in how one dresses, in rituals and ceremonies, in art and dance. In such cultures, illness, relationship issues and other forms of distress may be signs that a person has strayed too far from their personal power. The shaman might be called in help put the power animal back in us, and then we might be told to do rituals to keep the animal close, for example, to dance its dance every day.[71]

Process work also offers various ways to help people retrieve lost parts of the self. Process work calls parts that have been put aside marginalized, because they are located outside the person's identity. One useful route to reclaiming marginalized parts is through working on abuse issues, which may include physical, sexual, and emotional abuse, along with public humiliation. The trauma of these events often leads people to put aside important parts of the self, which are hard to reclaim without working through the original issue.

In both process work, where the individual does more of the work, and shamanism, where the shaman does most of it, the individual who was abused comes back feeling that they have regained access to parts of themselves that had been marginalized.

An important initial stage of abuse work involves telling the stories of what happened that was abusive. Telling the story often gives people access to memories and feelings that have been put aside. As these emotions are expressed, people may begin to experience relief from chronic body symptoms that are physical manifestations of the emotional experience of the abuse.

For example, I once worked with a woman who had terrible arm pain, which had been diagnosed as fibromyalgia. When she worked on this pain, she remembered two kinds of abuse. The first was that her mom had repeatedly grabbed her on those points on her arm. Through role-playing, she worked through her anger with her mom, and about 70% of the arm pain left and did not return. Another time she had a memory of being tied down after an operation, at these same points in her arm. She was cold and was trying to speak, but could not, due to the anesthesia; she also wanted to reach out for a blanket, but could not. When we went back and replayed this, she began to shake with cold, although it was a very hot day in my office. She worked through her anger in relation to the situation and had a chance to express everything she would have said if she had been able to speak after the operation. After that day, her arms were 100% pain free, despite the fact that her pain had previously been unbearable.

As people work further on abuse, a point may come where they need to not only reclaim emotions that have been put aside, but also qualities that they have come to associate with the abuser and therefore marginalized in themselves. For example, someone who was physically abused may try at all costs to avoid his or her own aggression, while a person who was sexually abused may avoid sexual expression. A person who was emotionally abused may marginalize the ability to be direct. People put a wall around the hurtful aspects of the abuser in an attempt never to act like the abuser. While this is an understandable reaction, it may backfire and marginalize parts of the person that they need. It's a little bit like having a poisoned well on a large piece of land. If we build a wall not only around the well, but many acres around it, then no one will ever get near the poisonous water. Let's say the land inside the wall has many productive fruit trees. If no one ever makes a gate in the wall and goes not to the well but to the rest of the land, then the fruit never gets eaten, and potential nourishment is lost.

Here's an example. Sherry and Ralph came in for therapy. Sherry had been severely sexually abused, and part of how she had coped with this was by picking a marriage partner who was not interested in sex. As a result of his own personal work, Ralph had become increasingly interested in sex and was beginning to put more sexual pressure on Sherry. One of Ralph's complaints was that Sherry never initiated sex. Sherry herself associated sexual initiation with the person who had sexually abused her and had never been interested in initiating sex. In addition, she wanted Ralph to initiate only in very low-key ways, since sexual excitement frightened her.

Sherry had come to a crisis in her identity. She loved Ralph and wanted to keep the marriage, but saw that he was beginning to drift away after years of sexual frustration, especially as his sexuality became more important to him.

Sherry wanted to be able to initiate, but her image of the initiator was so horrific that she couldn't imagine doing so. We worked slowly and carefully on this issue in therapy. Rather than going against Sherry's aversion to the initiator, we focused on adding a sense of playfulness to this role. Gradually, she was able to initiate sexual encounters with Ralph, always in a fun and playful way. She actually found that she didn't feel monstrous at all, but powerful in appropriate, adult ways. Sherry successfully retrieved the fruit from the trees behind the wall, and found great and unexpected pleasures in the fruits.

Here is another example of what can happen when a person picks up qualities they have marginalized because they associate these qualities with an abuser. John and Kate came in for marriage counseling. John was a logger and Kate's job was taking care of the children at home. She presented herself as a very strong, assertive woman who knew what she wanted. John seemed like a rough and tough person, especially when he talked about his profession as a logger. I expected Kate to complain about John being rough in their interactions, and was quite surprised when she complained about just the opposite. Kate was on the verge of leaving John because he refused to fight with her or stand up to her in any way at all. She felt that she could push him around and get anything she wanted. I told John that I was a bit surprised by this, because he seemed like such a tough guy. John agreed that he was tough in many areas, but not in his intimate relationships.

John then began to talk about his father, who had beaten John's mother and physically abused John. John had sworn that he would never be strong with his wife; he was trying to protect himself from becoming like his father, who had been so brutal throughout John's childhood. However, John had gotten into a bind; his wife found him so passive that she couldn't stand it any longer. Like Sherry in the example above, John had reached a crisis point. He did not want to lose his wife, but he could not imagine how to be strong in relationship without being abusive.

At this point in therapy, we took things slowly and talked a great deal about the difference between being assertive and being abusive. We tried to find men John knew who were able to use their assertiveness in positive ways. When John was able to make a few assertive statements, Kate began to smile widely. She told him how much this side of him excited her, both in general and sexually. John was thrilled with her reaction. During the time that John and Kate were in therapy, he took steps to begin becoming assertive. While he did not become the kind of partner Kate was looking for in terms of being met in conflict, his honest attempts sparked Kate's interest in him as her partner.

Facing Death with Equanimity

In the final stages of development relative to dying, people face death with equanimity. At this stage, death is not welcomed, but neither is it feared. Death is seen as part of the circle of life. People who have reached this stage are living so much in the moment that death, when it comes, is just another moment. People who are doing their life work until the last moment face death with the warrior sprit and sense of equanimity that many spiritual traditions refer to. I had a taste of this feeling after working in Israel. I had wanted to do conflict resolution work there for a long time and was thrilled to finally have the opportunity to do so. When I boarded the jet to return home, I was excited, exhausted, and full of positive feelings that I received from the experience.

While I am normally a bit anxious about flying on long journeys, I sat there with an incredible sense of peace. I was not ready to die, but this felt a glimpse of the peace that comes from doing something totally on one's path of heart.

Here is another example from my practice. Randy and I worked together for about six months before he died. Randy's rapid spiritual growth and intensive relationship work during this brief period completely changed my idea that it takes a long time to accept death with equanimity. Randy did not want to die and did not feel ready for death, but when the moment came, he died in peace with a smile on his face. His moment of death, which came just after he took part in a family ritual, seemed like a clear choice, and he died with full presence.

Dying with the full presence the Buddhists talk about requires living fully, since daily living is the practice ground for dying with our full awareness. When we go to our most important job interview, date, or art show, we bring as much of ourselves as we can muster. Dying is just another moment to which we can bring our full selves. I believe that we are all potential Zen Masters during our lives and at the moment of death. Death helps us get on with what we need to do in life, while life helps us learn what we need to know to face death. Life and death are parts of the same wheel. In this place of non-duality, there is no need to be terrified of either life or death, any more than we need to fear spring becoming summer or fall becoming winter. All the seasons, life and death, are parts of the same dance.

While the feeling states associated with this final stage are similar to those in the previous stage, there is a significant difference. In the stage of living fully, the primary emotions are happiness and peacefulness. Much of this happiness is tied to what our accomplishments are and the ecstasy of doing tasks on one's life path. In the final stages of facing death with equanimity, all emotions and experience are welcomed, and in the background is a sense of enlightenment and detachment from the whole drama of life. The main feeling associated with this state is one of growing peace and acceptance of one's life. There is often more awareness and caring about the world as a whole. While the happiness of the living fully stage is more associated with doing, the happiness of facing death with equanimity is more associated with being all of one's self.

Summary

In this chapter, we have seen that there are various core attitudes toward life and death, which range from not caring, to being tied to the wheel, developing detachment, living more fully, and approaching life and death with equanimity. While our core attitude toward life and death often comes from childhood, an individual can develop through all the stages in order to face life and death with joy and detachment.

EXERCISE: Core Attitudes toward Living and Dying

1. Sit and meditate. Think for a moment about the family you grew up in. Which of the five attitudes toward living and dying best describes them? Did they not care about living and dying? Were they tied to the wheel, becoming detached, living fully, or facing death with equanimity?

2. Next, think about which of these five attitudes best describes your current attitude toward living and dying.

3. Imagine that you could move momentarily to either living fully or facing death with equanimity as a basic attitude towards life. What would you need to let go of or work through to get to this place? Perhaps it is some attachment to a part of your life, or unfinished business with a parent or other person in your life.
4. Pretend for a little while that you are actually at living fully and / or facing death with equanimity. What, if anything, is relieving about being here? What if anything, makes you feel a bit uncomfortable?
5. Do you somehow need more of this new position in your present life? How would your current life be different if you incorporated more of this position?

| CHAPTER 9 |

Modern Medicine

What strikes me about our system is that more people are afraid of how they are going to die than the fact that they are going to die. How did the medical profession get to where people are so afraid of us?[72]

This chapter was difficult for me to write, because my experience with traditional modern medicine is widely varied. I come from a family of many doctors who are dedicated, loving people and wonderful medical practitioners. Many of my close friends are physicians who were called to the profession by a deep desire to help and serve people. I am impressed by the amazing technology of modern medicine. In addition, based on my own experiences, the experiences of my clients, and the way I see doctors treated, both at medical school and by hospitals and the insurance companies, that our modern medical system is seriously ill.

In *Jewish Reflections on Death*, Jack Reimer notes some of the difficulties that face modern medical doctors:

> For doctors who have been trained to fight to save and enhance life, each patient's death is a kind of defeat, and so it is understandable that they find it hard to accept. Doctors are

> faced with the unhappy choice of either becoming accustomed to death so that they can survive emotionally the strain of their work and thereby becoming callous, or else of letting themselves be torn apart by feelings of failure and grief and guilt with each patient whom they lose.[73]

Unfortunately, the modern medical system often creates as much suffering as it brings healing. Some of this suffering is physical and iatrogenic, or brought about by medical treatment. Here, I wish to focus on the psychological suffering caused by the fact that the medical system benefits economically from fear. In some ways, each of us is responsible for the perpetuation of this system. All of us, whether we are doctors, patients, or both, can demand change and use our influence to move the system.

Technicians vs. Healers

In my experience, most doctors are called to their profession by the desire to heal people. Without such a goal, it would be hard to endure the difficulties involved in becoming and being a doctor. Unfortunately, few doctors seem to feel or act like healers once they are practicing. I believe that this is due to the modern medical system, which trains the desire to heal out of physicians and demands that they be technicians rather than healers.

In my definition, a healer is someone who treats the whole person, including not only the body, but also the psyche. A true healer heals not only with technical skills, but also with their presence. Until our medical system can address the whole person, so that not only the body but also the psyche is healthier after seeking treatment, then we have a system where physicians are not true healers. In most cases, the best one can hope for when dealing with a modern medical doctor is to find a highly skilled technician.

Philosophically, a technician supports the "tied to the wheel" phase of life. A technician keeps a person going and provides reassurance that they are not yet dead. In contrast, the healer helps a person embrace life and death regardless of how close they are to dying. The technician views death and the altered or comatose states that often precede death as signs of failure. A healer embraces death as part of nature and helps guide people through the natural stages before death.

Our current Western medical system, which tries to shorten medical visits, for insurance purposes, to a few minutes, does not foster healing relationships. Modern medicine, which relies increasingly on test results rather than on the physician's experience and the intuition of client and physician, does not foster collaboration or empowerment for doctors or patients. Many times tests are run not primarily because the patient's condition requires the test, but because there is some slight possibility that needs to be tested for so that the physician will not be open to a possible lawsuit. Also, doing the interview and examination method to determine the complexity of a situation often takes more time than a test.

In addition, to be a healer, one must have time to maintain one's own personal power of healing. Most of the physicians I know have been trained in medical school to minimize their own needs. In the June 11, 2000 issue of the Register Guard, a Eugene, Oregon newspaper, there was an article talking about medical school training. In a review of programs, 36% of general surgery, 54% of pediatric, 30% of internal medicine violated standards about how they work their medical students. "Reviewers found frequent violations of three standards in particular. The standards state that residents must have off at least one day out of every seven, should not be on duty in the hospital more often than every third night and should not have to work more than a specified number of hours averaged over a one-month period."[74] Stopping violations like this will help protect the medical students, and protect all of us who are their patients. Anyway that medical school dehumanizes their students costs all of us in the potential quality of treatment and personal care we receive. Working too many hours and other kinds of violations like this can contribute to creating a numbed out effect on the student that can carry over into how they later practice. They have been taught to live with sleep deprivation and without exercise. They often fail to balance work with other parts of lives. The physicians I know often suffer terribly from lack of time and attention for their families, including their relationship partners. I remember being at a dinner gathering with a whole table of doctors. One of the doctors was paged and went to the telephone to return the call. His wife told me that in all their years of marriage, he had never been present during an entire dinner out. This high level of overwork and stress takes a toll on physicians' bodies, relationships, and spirits. The modern medical system makes it nearly impossible for physicians to heal themselves.

Think back for a moment to the presence of doctors you have seen. How many them inspire you to be healthy and feel good about yourself, simply by their presence? Here is an example. My wife and I took our young daughter to see a doctor because she had fallen off a slide and we thought she had broken her wrist. The doctor walked in. Without saying hello to my daughter, my wife, or me, he grabbed our young child's arm. In turn, I grabbed his arm and said, "Excuse me, but before you grab her, how about saying hello? We have never met you." The doctor looked stunned. He sat down and we had a talk. It turned out he was friends with a good friend of mine, and the rest of the visit was a pleasure. He did a great job medically and was warm and caring as a person. Something about our modern medical system dehumanizes both physicians and patients to the point that this pediatrician, a warm and caring individual, would neglect to greet his patients.

This is not by any means an isolated example. On the average, I hear people's horror stories about poor medical treatment at least several times each month. I have heard stories about people who were given medicine that almost killed them, even after they alerted the physician to this information. One person's physician told them to go home and die rather than bothering the doctor. I have had clients who were over-tested and overmedicated and clients who begged physicians to take their complaints seriously while they suffered unnecessarily.

My friends who are homeopaths have told me that the homeopathic approach to medicine says that we swallow not only the pill, but also the person who prescribes it. They have extrapolated this conclusion from anecdotal evidence from their clients. Many clients note that they go to one homeopath who gives them a remedy that doesn't work. They might then go to another homeopath who gives them the same remedy, which then does work. Apparently this common experience in homeopathy led them to the conclusion that it is not just the remedy, but the person giving the remedy that matters.

Here is a related example from my practice. One of my clients called her physician's office in the middle of the night because she was having chest pains and other possible symptoms of heart problems after undergoing chemotherapy. She couldn't get through to the office, and in a moment of panic, she called the doctor at home. He cussed her out, told her to take some aspirin, and hung up on her. At another time, this same doctor told her she wouldn't have medical problems if she weren't "such a fatty." His attitude was far from healing, yet he was a brilliant technician who helped save this woman's life. However, she also "swallowed" his abusive attitude, and needed lots of therapeutic assistance to undo the emotional damage he did to her.

I have seen many people whose symptoms become far worse after abusive or painful relationship interactions. Stories such as the one above underscore our desperate need for a medical system that supports doctors to be whole people rather than just technicians.

Process-Oriented Attitudes Towards Symptoms

I remember once coming into Arnold Mindell's office when I had a cold, the first one I'd had in years. He told me that this was very exciting. At the time, I was shocked, since I was less than excited by my cold symptoms. In retrospect, I can see that his comment reflected a very different attitude than we find in either alternative or traditional medicine.

From a process-oriented standpoint, a body symptom is simply the body's way of expressing something dreamlike. From this perspective, a symptom is an exciting as well as a painful or difficult experience. If we believe that symptoms are the body's way of trying to communicate with us, we feel that there is something right, meaningful, or useful about our symptoms. This meaning-based philosophy does not exist in traditional or alternative medical approaches. In contrast, the central principle behind modern medicine is all illness is wrong. From this perspective, symptoms should be eliminated or repressed by drugs, surgery, radiation, chemotherapy, and other methods.

The attitude that we have about symptoms has a significant impact on us. The next time you feel sick, try this experiment with a friend. First, have your friend tell you that something must be wrong with you because you have a symptom. Then have them tell you to believe in what is happening, that it is meaningful, and that they will help you discover what nature wants in this moment. Notice the different reactions you have to each of these approaches. Simply telling a person that something is wrong with him or her is has a powerful hypnotic impact that leaves the person agreeing that something is wrong. If we follow the process-oriented theory that symptoms are dreamlike communications from the body and nature, then we will take a more encouraging view of the symptom. Such encouragement may help bring issues to the surface, allowing the person more options for working with the symptom.

Here is an example. Fran, who is suffering from chronic fatigue syndrome, comes in for her first session. I tell her that I am interested in her condition and that, while I know how painful it can be, I have helped many people find meaning and healing in their chronic fatigue. Fran is already relieved and says that many practitioners don't like working with chronic fatigue. My genuine sympathy, interest, and hope are the right medicine to launch an exploration of what chronic fatigue means in Fran's life. Eventually, she was able to move out of her fatigue in a way that might not have been possible if she did not have access to the potential meaning in her symptom.

In contrast to modern medicine, which has a goal of repressing symptoms, process work tries to increase awareness of what is happening in a symptom. One basic principle of process work with symptoms is that amplifying a symptom may help the deeper meaning behind it to emerge. Here is an example. Paul had had shoulder problems for many years. He had gone to many traditional and alternative medical practitioners without finding any relief. Instead of trying to eliminate the symptom, I asked him to amplify the way his shoulder pain made him stand. As Paul gradually exaggerated his posture, he suddenly started to walk like a monster. He took heavy steps and growled. We discovered an enormous power hidden in his shoulder symptom. After we found this power, I role-played Paul's ordinary self in order to explore what the newly discovered power might want. We discovered that the "monster" was after him because Paul needed to be more powerful in his relationship and at work. The dialogue between Paul and the monstrous power in his shoulders went on for quite a while. After this work, Paul was able to move freely for the first time in years.

I have seen that working with symptoms in this way often brings out unknown parts of us. For most people, having a symptom is like having a long-term guest living in the house; a guest that we never stop to talk with. Once we find out what the symptom is about, and if we can do what the symptom asks of us, the original symptom often disappears.

Here is another example. During a lecture I was giving at a college, a woman in the audience asked for a demonstration of process work with symptoms. When I asked if she had any symptoms, she said that she could barely lift her arm. I asked her to put her arm right at the point where she could not move it further, and then to amplify how her arm looked and felt and moved at that stuck place. As she put her arm in this position, she had a sudden realization that her arm didn't work well exactly at the spot where her husband had his own arm amputated. She exclaimed that his left arm and her left arm were dreaming together. When I asked her if she felt she had to suffer with her husband, she cried and said that she didn't really feel free to have her own sense of life. I asked her to imagine for a moment that she were free, and didn't have to live as a duplicate of her husband. She began to move her arm and was shocked to realize that not only could she raise her arm, but that she could also swing it around her head. Getting to the bottom of the emotions behind her arm pain provided her instant relief. All her pain pills and other treatments had not provided relief because they didn't really address her problems.

Process work with symptoms is not always so immediate, but people usually do get in touch with deep parts of themselves during such work. While this type of work may not necessarily relieve the original symptom, it often provides a sense of immediate excitement. Fear about what is wrong is usually replaced by the thrill of self-discovery.

I don't mean to imply that repressing symptoms does not work. Sometimes symptoms can be repressed with no side effects, even if a person doesn't get in touch with a deeper meaning behind the symptom. Sometimes it is right to repress a symptom rather than to work on it. At these times, repression works well.

However, if a symptom is trying to communicate something crucial to a person, when the symptoms are eliminated, they either tend to come back, or another symptom immediately appears. Strings of symptoms may indicate that the body is dreaming, providing one symptom after another in hopes that the person will get the message.

Traditional medical approaches and process-oriented approaches can work quite well together. For example, let's say that a person has a painful non-cancerous growth. They work on the symptom, which leads them to all kinds of insights and transformations, and the symptom remains. At a certain point, the pain gets worse and worse, so the person decides to go for surgery, which goes remarkably well. In fact, the person's recovery rate is so rapid that the surgeons even bring other doctors to check it out. I have seen cases like this many times, in fact, so often that I have come to believe that working on a symptom before and after surgery can have a very positive impact on healing.

Similarly, at a time when traditional or alternative medical treatments are not working well, processing the symptom can help the treatments become more effective again. For example, I was working with a woman who went to a chiropractor because she was experiencing a lot of back pain. After a chiropractic adjustment, her back stayed aligned for a few days, and then went out again. We worked on this experience from a process work standpoint and discovered that her normal identity was to be linear and tight and conservative, while another part of her wanted to step out and become more unconventional. We did this in the session by having her make movements she would not normally make. She began to suddenly swing her arms wildly over her head, and made jumps and other spontaneous movements. We talked about other parts of her life where she would like to be more spontaneous and free. After this work, she had an adjustment from her chiropractor, which lasted for several months. One way to look at this is that her back didn't need to go out because instead her whole self was stepping out. Her back could stay aligned because she picked up the process of stepping out of her line of acceptable behavior.

What works to heal a person is highly individual. Sometimes process work alone is enough. Sometimes traditional or alternative medicine alone may suffice. Sometimes a combination is effective, and sometimes doing nothing is the best medicine. I believe that as our medical system opens to the concept that healing is an individual process and that meaning is hidden in symptoms, people will suffer far less from their symptoms, and interventions will work much better. Through honoring, amplifying, and finding the meaning of symptoms, we are saying to nature that we honor and follow her.

When we follow nature, the level of fear around medical treatment tends to drop dramatically. Terror around medical treatment may come partly because we know that traditional medical treatment is not necessarily right for our whole selves; we may know that a mainstream solution works only when it is right for the individual's process. Other parts of us may become scared because they know that the medical system is against them and will work to repress them. Many of these parts have a hard enough time coming forward; when they finally emerge in a symptom, everyone is against them and wants to get rid of them.

For example, let's go back to Paul and his shoulder problem. Paul is against his power coming out, so it shows itself in his symptom and makes him walk a bit like a monster. This is the dreaming process peaking out and expressing itself. But now that it has emerged, it is labeled as a symptom, and everyone wants to get rid of the symptom without relating to the monster. This is scary, even to the monstrous parts of ourselves. They need a place to live, and when unfolded and developed, as we saw in Paul's example, they usually transform into important, interesting parts of our personalities. If we can keep this open attitude long enough to explore what is trying to emerge in symptoms, we may be able to greatly decrease our fear of symptoms and of medical intervention.

Breaking the Hypnosis

Both mainstream and alternative medical approaches share the unspoken hypnosis that illness is inevitable. This hypnosis includes the assumption that certain symptoms or illnesses are inevitable, along with the assumption that an illness will take the same course in any person.

Here is an example of the hypnosis that illness and symptoms are inevitable. I went to an alternative physician because I was very anxious about a symptom. While he assured me that I was currently in good health, he said that within a few years my symptoms would increase, because most people develop additional problems as they age. When I commented that he had just made a hypnotic suggestion that I would get ill, he didn't know what I was talking about. This doctor's attitude is almost unavoidable in our medical systems, which are based on statistics and which also see people as fitting into statistical patterns more than as individuals with their own processes around illness and healing. A doctor's suggestion that a person is ill is so powerful that people can end up developing symptoms based on what the physician finds predictable.

Dr. Andrew Weil calls this medical hexing. He is working to help medical schools incorporate training doctors to take extreme care with the words they use. He says that it is crucial to ensure that doctors become more conscious with the power they carry. He notes that physicians need to have more awareness of giving the power back in ways that influence health for better rather than for worse, that stimulate rather than retard spontaneous healing.[75]

He goes on to say, " The usual effect of a medical hex is despair, and I cannot believe that despair has beneficial effects on the human healing system. It is not a good idea to stay in treatment with a doctor who thinks you cannot get better."[76]

Most people have individual experiences that do not go along with the medical hypnosis about the course of an illness and what one needs to do to heal. For example, my childhood pediatrician always prescribed rest for a cold or the flu. He not only wanted me to rest until I felt better, and also told me not to do any athletic activities for an additional week. Since I loved sports, this was very hard for me. Partially out of rebellion, I discovered that I could kick certain illnesses almost instantly by going home and doing exercises. I also learned to control my body temperature to a certain degree. When I woke up with a fever, my mother would say that I had to go to the doctor if I still had a fever at 11 A.M. When she took my temperature, more often than not, I had been able to reduce the fever by the methods I had discovered.

My methods relied heavily on visualization. I would picture something attacking the germs, or forces rallying my strength. In my visualization, I would call in armies of allies to fight what was making me sick. These techniques are similar to Dr. Carl Simonton's creative visualizations, in which he had people visualize something attacking their cancer cells.[77] Another thing I always did was get up and move. My doctor always told me not to exercise, insisting that I should avoid all sports for a week, even if I had only a simple cold. I always went home from his office and followed my body. Sometimes this meant resting, or sometimes I did jumping jacks and other intense exercises. Several times, I brought about quick cures doing exercises—the illnesses left me immediately.

Process work has similar methods of working with symptoms. One method of working with symptoms is to tell people to follow what is happening in their bodies. Movement processes often come out of experiencing a symptom. One time I was working with a woman on a childhood experience. She suddenly started to have an asthma attack, which she hadn't had since she was a child. Before I asked her what we should do medically, she leapt up and started a wild dance. Not only did the asthma disappear, she suddenly felt energy return to her that she hadn't felt in years. Her chronic low energy state was gone. This experience was the beginning of her picking up lots of energy, which led to numerous life changes. These methods, developed independently by different practitioners, work because the body is more than a physical machine. The body dreams, and any time we do something symbolic, or do something to follow ourselves, we enter the dreaming level. My repeated experience, and the theory of process work, says that entering into dreaming can be very important to the person to sustain their good health.

Occasionally, a medical practitioner is open to individual experiences. For example, I went to an amazing root canal specialist several years ago. He was a remarkable technician and was able to fix a problem that had caused me pain for a year. At that appointment, he found additional problems in a different tooth. He explained that, due to another dentist's error in misplacing a post, I had bone loss in my jaw. He said that the chances of saving the tooth were very slim, as bone does not regenerate. Since he seemed open-minded, I asked him to try repeating the chances of saving the tooth in a way that left some room for my own individual nature. He completely reformulated his prediction and said that while some people have trouble regenerating bone, I had my own way, and he was open to waiting and seeing what happened with the tooth. In six months, I had regenerated so much bone that his probe couldn't find the huge pocket that was once there.

Whenever professionals tell people statistics around healing, they program, to a certain extent, what will happen to that person. A healer, who uses statistics to indicate what some people's experiences will be, and also stays open to individual experience, creates a pathway of possibility for the client. A true healer knows that anything is possible around healing, and is interested in the mystical worlds beyond the fixed and known. In contrast, a technician who only knows the known path may unconsciously limit their patients' healing experience to the known realm. For example, I once had a client who had cancer. He felt that his oncologist really cared about him and would come back from his oncology appointments full of life and hope and determination to keep going. One day his doctor was away, and he saw a different oncologist. This doctor told my client that it was a waste of time for him to keep coming back, as he was going to die soon anyway. When my client came to see me after this appointment, he was so upset, that he was considering suicide. This example shows how much difference the human element makes—the human connection may at times make a life and death difference.

Dr. Andrew Weil sums up the negative medical hypnosis when he says, "Simply put: too many doctors are deeply pessimistic about the possibility of people getting better; they communicate their pessimism to patients and their families.[78]

Weil also provides a clear example of how this hypnosis works in action. In his example, a urologist has just told a patient that they will die soon. In Weil's words,

> A high priest of technological medicine, enthroned in his temple, had uttered the equivalent of a shaminstic curse, for doctors in our culture are invested with the very same power others project onto shamans and priests. Those words were the source of the patient's terror, a terror that paralyzed him and prevented him from making constructive efforts for his own survival and well being.[79]

Weil points out that the way physicians treat people can actually make them a dangerous force in people's lives. Even when their technical expertise is helpful, their messages and communication style may create terror, unless a person somehow develops the inner strength to believe in their own wisdom rather than the doctor's prediction. Weil says of his patients that, "many have suffered physically, emotionally, or financially as a result of encounters with conventional medicine."[80]

I believe that we may have put our faith in false gods by putting so much weight on the opinions of medical professionals. Our fear of illness and death may not only be about illness and death, but in part about the medical system and the negative hypnosis that is pervasive throughout it. If this is true, then a partial answer to our fears is to empower ourselves to participate in our own healing, not only by seeking out the healers that work for us, but also through getting in touch with our own internal healers. Since we have been trained not to pay attention to our own internal knowledge, it can take a lifetime to truly get back in touch with our own sense of healing.

For example, when I had digestive troubles in my late teens, I went to many different doctors, who gave me more and more medicine, which had no effect on me at all. In my early twenties, I went out of town to attend a personal growth center. I changed my diet. I learned to freely express my feelings. Most of my digestive problems disappeared. Within each of us is an amazing healer, and following our own sense of what is right for us is often the best prescription for wellness.

At this growth center, before I knew the formal techniques of process work, whenever I felt ill I tried simply to feel what was happening inside me in detail. When I paid attention, I noticed that spontaneous feelings, movements, and wild fantasies emerged. As I spent time in these different spaces, strangely enough, sometimes fevers disappeared and pains and injuries went away. I was on the journey to regain my own inner healer.

This was the first time in my life that I was more interested in feeling well and healing myself than in being a good boy who went to the doctor. I was learning that sometimes the doctor's suggestions fit with my experience, and at these times, they would be likely to help. I was also starting to notice what happened when I had been hexed or cursed by the negative hypnosis and pessimism of the practitioner. At these times, I found ways to undo the suggestions and patterning that might program me towards illness and inhibit my own potential to heal.

In my experience and in what I have seen with many clients, going to the doctor has become like going to the priest or the rabbi, to church or temple. Often, we are so programmed to listen to external advice about ourselves and our health, that we no longer listen to our own bodies, no longer consider that we may have the answer within. We may even feel guilty when we start to listen to our intuitions about what we need to heal, similar to feeling guilt about doubting a religious teaching.

Many medical schools are now trying to put the human element back into healthcare, as the technical aspects of medicine have been so overemphasized. We have seen that some medical specialists now talk about how doctors program people's healing by what they say, and call for treatment that is more personal. The message is starting to get through. One by one, doctors and patients are waking up to the limits and problems of the medical system, and are beginning to feel free enough to speak out for change.

Bringing an Interest in Process Back to Medicine

Medical schools are beginning to teach students about the art of the intake interview again, as a regular part of their training. Students are trained to try to hear more about who the person is and to understand the symptom in the context of that person. Such an interview is the beginning of taking an interest in the whole person, discovering what their waking life is like, what their dreams are about.

Doing such an interview requires not only interest in the person but also time to sit with them. Andrew Weil proposes an interesting solution to the time dilemma, as our current mainstream medical system does not allow doctors the time to sit with a patient and discover what their life is like. He suggests that for most problems, people don't need a traditional mainstream practitioner. In his vision, people could see alternative practitioners for most health problems, and seek out traditional medical care only for emergencies and acute serious illnesses.[81]

There are also other signs that the system of training doctors is changing. According to an article in the The Register-Guard, the Eugene, Oregon newspaper, the number of medical schools that now contain courses that deal with spirituality and medicine is up to 60 of the nation's 128 medical schools. Susan Vangarck, from the National Center for Complementary and Alternative Medicine, offers these statistics, and says, "The Hippocratic Oath calls for treating the whole person, not just a symptom or specific aliment."[82]

Alternative practitioners tend to encompass more of this holistic perspective. Seeing alternative practitioners for many health problems is a good idea. However, I wish to point out that the negative medical hypnosis is by no means limited to mainstream practitioners. Many alternative practitioners take on the role of "expert" and believe that patients will not be healthy without seeing the doctor regularly. I believe that practitioners of all sorts need to shift their focus toward helping people connect with their own internal ability to heal. Over reliance on a practitioner of any sort, combined with negative hypnotic statements, contributes to the feeling of powerlessness and lack of control that many people experience in the medical system. My experience is that any type of medical intervention works far better when a person's unique process is considered and followed.

Shelly's story is a good example of how considering the whole person's process is helpful in healing. When Shelly came to see me for therapy, she told the following story. She had such debilitating headaches that she was referred to a neurologist and diagnosed with a brain tumor. She had surgery, and the tumor, which was benign, was completely removed. After the surgery, her symptoms became worse. She went back to the doctor many times, and the doctor only said that the surgery was successful and that Shelly could not possibly be having the symptoms she was experiencing. Meanwhile, Shelly's headaches continued to get worse. One day, Shelly came in and jokingly said that she would probably feel fine if she got out of her marriage. As she had suffered so much in her marriage, I told her to pretend for one week that she was divorced. Surprisingly, Shelly's headaches disappeared immediately. She eventually left her husband and continued to live free of headaches. In Shelly's case, did her headaches come from a brain tumor that needed removing, a husband that needed removing, or both? The technician is interested only in the tumor, but the healer follows all aspects of the individual and stays open minded to healing from all directions.

The Medical Environment as Terrifying

We have seen thus far that the attitude and negative hypnotic statements of mainstream medicine can be terrifying for people. Another source of fear is the physical environment that one normally finds in a medical setting. In most hospitals and nursing homes, the physical atmosphere is like a temple to technology. The clothing hospital patients are required to wear are usually ugly and humiliating, while hospital food makes many people feel ill. Stimulus in patient rooms and waiting rooms comes only from television, and visiting hours are rarely designed to fit patients' needs. In an inpatient environment, people sometimes wait days to see the doctor.

Going to see a regular practitioner on an outpatient basis can be a similar experience. The most healing aspect about waiting several weeks, then several hours, to see your practitioner for a few minutes, may be that it provides an opportunity to work on one's anger about the system. For example, in Eugene, if you have a skin problem, to get into see most dermatologists takes about six weeks, while seeing another type of specialist usually takes about a month. The average wait at the pediatric clinic, with an appointment, is over an hour. Unfortunately, the delay most people experience before seeing the doctor only makes them more frightened. Our current medical system, which expects people to give up a great deal of their time to see a busy physician for just a few minutes, makes most people feel devalued.

In a few places, the medical system is beginning to shift the structure that devalues patients and elevates doctors. For example, there is a hospital, Shands Hospital in Gainesville, Florida, which is based on art and medicine.[83] In this hospital, the physical surroundings are beautiful—healing in a place that feels like an art gallery is very different from trying to heal in a typical hospital room. The patients and doctors do various art projects together, and even the critical care wards are full of artwork. People are creative up to the moment of their death, and both doctors and patients talk about how much they enjoy their experience. This type of structure helps to level the difference of status between doctors and patients.

I have also visited a nursing home based on holistic ideas. The nursing home is called Hayes Valley Care and is located in San Francisco. For similar cost to a traditional nursing home, people enjoy beautiful rooms, a gourmet restaurant that is also open to the public, and many alternative activities. This type of setting helps the people living there feel that they are still participating in the pleasures of daily life. I spoke to several patients who were doing far better than they had in other settings, with no other differences than a change in environment. Creating attractive physical environments, adjusting scheduling so people don't have to wait more than fifteen minutes to see their practitioner, and introducing a focus on creativity may do more for healing than the next hundred medicines approved by the FDA.

The Healing Power of People

Creating attractive, collaborative healthcare settings is one way to level the playing field between healthcare professionals and patients. In addition, the power of human interaction goes a long way. Here is an example from National Public Radio. In a hospital with two different floors for cancer patients, people consistently seemed to recover faster and live longer on one floor than on the other. The hospital began all kinds of studies to find out why. They studied air quality, nursing care, and explored many other variables. They concluded that everything on both floors was the same, except that there was an almost legendary cleaning woman on the floor where everyone got so much better. While cleaning each room, she talked to people about getting better, telling them how much she loved them, and praying for them. This woman's presence was the only difference all the studies could find. More love for patients may be a missing piece in healing—a piece we will never find under even the most powerful microscope. Shamans know that much of the magic in their healing comes from the relationship and connection between healer and practitioner. The technical cure serves more to give the patient a physical anchor to a healing process that occurs in other realms.

When people talk about their fears of illness, they often bring up images of sterile hospital scenes. This imagery needs to change, since it creates unnecessary fear that compromises healing. Imagine visiting a beautiful setting to see a practitioner leading a healthy lifestyle that radiates to you. This practitioner is interested in your symptoms as they fit your whole being, and is interested in following what works for you as far as healing options. This is an experience that most people would look forward to rather than fear. We can create this kind of experience in a traditional medical setting. For example, I remember visiting a mainstream doctor was when I was in my early twenties. I was generally nervous at that time. My living situation was stressful and I was far away from home for the first time in my life. The doctor told me I shouldn't come in so often, and that instead, I should learn to trust nature more. I still remember his kind eyes and the way her put his hand on my shoulder when he spoke me. This doctor was both a good technician and a healer. He saw into me and knew what I really needed.

Andrew Weil, who is an expert on integrating traditional and alternative medicine, states clearly the importance of the physician and patient remembering that the real healing powers lie within the individual. He notes that, "Even when treatments are applied with successful outcomes, those outcomes represent activation of intrinsic healing mechanisms, which, under other circumstances, might operate without any outside stimulus. The body can heal itself. It can do so because it has a healing system."[84]

Love, Fear and Medicine

Do you remember the story about the cleaning woman whose caring presence was determined to contribute to higher cure rates in a cancer ward? We don't need elaborate studies to know that feeling loved helps us heal. Do you remember how it felt falling off your bike and scraping your knee, and how the kind hugs and loving words of your parents made it all better? There are parts of us that express our need to be loved through our anxieties and physical symptoms. In our current medical system, few people feel that there is sufficient time and relationship for their doctor to actually love and care about them.

Due to my work with people in comatose states, I spend a fair amount of time in hospitals. In my observation, the nurses, physical therapists, speech therapists, occupational therapists, and family members provide the caring and loving energy for the patient. In most cases, the doctor is quite distant from the everyday caring interaction around the patient. However, the status and the rank that doctors have make their caring, information, and time important. The current system creates a conflict between time, money and production on one side and caring and relationship on the other side.

Medical schools often teach doctors to create distance between themselves and their patients. This style has benefits and disadvantages for both patient and physician. The upside is that the doctor can function without being on a constant emotional roller coaster in situations where there is little time to process feelings. In the hectic environment of a hospital, finding time to eat lunch is enough of a challenge; there is no time for a physician to focus on feelings about a patient who just died. The disadvantage for physicians is that cutting oneself off from emotions creates poor mental and emotional health not only for the doctors but also for their families. If a person shuts down emotionally to survive at work, it is hard to simply open back up when one comes home to a partner or children after work.

Another difficulty for physicians is that spending time with people who are in poor health can be hard on the caregiver's own body and feelings. I know this difficulty well from my own practice. Unlike most doctors, I often have the luxury of the time and training to clear out anything I may pick up from my clients. Here is an example. Sandy came in for her session. She had been in extreme pain from migraine headaches and was desperate for relief, as no medical approach she had tried was helping. While she was talking about her pain, I noticed that my head started to hurt a bit on the right side. I asked her if this was where she often had pain, and she said yes, that that was the exact spot. Then I took a moment to explore the painful sensation in my head. I remembered that just before my head started to hurt, I had a feeling towards Sandy that I pushed aside. I was feeling a great deal of sadness for the suffering she had in her life. When I told Sandy the feeling, my head felt fine again, and the exchange took Sandy and me to a whole new place in our relationship. For the first time she really felt that I understood what she was going through. She felt my compassion for her, and we were able to work at new levels of openness about what was really behind all the pain in her life that was manifesting in her migraines. By feeling a drop of her pain, I was seen as a compassionate feeling witness to her pain. I also picked up on the signals of pain because Sandy never spoke about her own pain about life, just the pain in her head. After this session, she was more able to identify with the pain in her life and the needs she has for sympathy, compassion, and understanding.

Doctors aren't usually given the skills, time and permission to explore their feelings toward patients; in fact they are often taught to ignore these feelings. This means that doctors are left with unprocessed feelings and reactions that may have body components for themselves and their patients. A body component means that feelings and experiences that are meaningful and important to us, and that we don't bring into our awareness, may instead show up as body experiences. This is a way our body stores information. Sometimes these are little symptoms, like feeling very tired after being with a certain patient, or a bit upset. Sometimes, if these reactions and feelings are repeatedly marginalized, a more significant symptom may appear.

For example, a friend of mine was not able to set limits with a particular client who was in distress. She kept him at home for counseling with her crises, and he couldn't stop thinking about her situation. Eventually, he stopped being able to sleep well, and then started experiencing stress symptoms. When he worked on this and was finally able to set a limit, and tell her how he could be available and how not, his symptoms disappeared. He first had to process this on a body, or symptom level, and then eventually was able to bring it up as a therapeutic issue.

Doctors and other helping professionals have an increased chance of developing physical symptoms as a result of their unprocessed emotions. In addition, if a physician is not trained to bring in feelings, the patient misses out on the valuable clues about their symptoms that the physician may pick up through their own body and emotions. Finally, the patient may experience a doctor who has been trained to repress feelings about patients as cold and uncaring.

Since there is no way to prevent health care professionals, who are human, from having feelings about and reactions to patients, we need a better way to work with these feelings. One option is for medical schools to start training physicians in how to process their feelings towards patients. This could be accomplished in physician support groups, as inner work at home, and internally while the doctor works with the patient. For example, sometimes I stop during a therapy session and say I need a minute for myself. I can process my reactions internally and keep my own body clear, or I may decide to share certain emotions or awareness with my client. It is important not to make a program out of sharing, any more than it is useful to make a program out of detaching or numbing. Both are appropriate at times, and the key is to develop the fluidity to use whichever is fitting in the moment.

The detachment that many medical schools train their doctors to maintain can be extremely useful if used consciously at certain moments. For example, there are times when a physician just has to act without feeling much, such as while doing emergency heart surgery. It may be important for the doctor to drop their feeling towards the person and just carry out the task. However, at another moment, having these feelings may be just the ticket, such as when dealing with a patient who is struggling with cancer. The physicians caring for the person can greatly inspire the person to keep fighting the cancer.

Summary

While modern medicine has made great leaps in terms of technology, this growth has sometimes been at the cost of the healing aspects of medicine. The system has demanded that physicians and hospitals focus more on illnesses than on people. The resulting rebellion against this technical approach has resulted in many people choosing to use alternative medicine. However, alternative medical approaches are not necessarily alternative in terms of how they view people and the interpersonal aspects of treatment.

This chapter has called for a new kind of medicine that uses technology as necessary, but which is also more process, dreaming, and person-based. The costs of the current time-pressured system are felt not only by patients, but also by physicians. Change needs to happen, starting with more humane treatment of doctors in training. Doctors need to be taught how to process their feelings and their own physical symptoms, particularly those that come up while working with patients. To restore healing, we all need to change our language about and approach to symptoms. Rather than considering a symptom as wrong, we need to see symptoms as something meaningful trying to happen. Changing the physical environment of healthcare settings to a more nurturing atmosphere would be immensely helpful. Becoming aware of alternative approaches is important. Physicians need to become aware of how they program clients' experiences. Finally, we all need to become aware of the power that love and caring have to heal. Our own inner healers need to be supported, trained, and awakened, so that we do not project the ability to heal only outwardly on physicians. All of us are responsible for these changes happening.

I have been critical of the Western mainstream medical system in various ways during this chapter. However, I want to end with several notes of hope. More and more doctors and medical schools are incorporating alternative medical techniques such as homeopathy, herbal medicine, shamanism, acupuncture, and other methods. As consumers demand more holistic care and back up their demands with where they spend their treatment dollars, the system is forced to change. Hospice nurses, who seem to have an extraordinary openness to all kinds of physical and spiritual healing, have transformed the hospice movement and often spread their acceptance to the doctors they work with. Body-mind approaches continue to influence medicine, as more doctors study alternative psychology. Alternative approaches such as Process-Oriented Psychology are also learning to address the concerns of mainstream medicine by incorporating standardized research methods into techniques such as coma work.

The revolution in medicine is moving in the direction of more humane treatment. Rebellion against medical care that doesn't feel right, or do right, for the patient, is spreading among doctors and patients alike. The patients' bill of rights was a hot issue before the Congress of 1999. Hopefully this movement toward change will continue to work for the betterment of physicians and patients together.

EXERCISE (This exercise requires two people)

1. Imagine the kind of doctor you would like to visit. What kind of setting do they work in? How do they walk, dress, act, stand, how do they use their hands, what is their mind and energy like? Let your creativity and imagination have fun with this vision.

2. Once you have a clear image of this doctor, experiment with becoming him / her. As your helper plays you, see how you as the doctor would treat one of your symptoms.

3. Now come back and be yourself. Let the other person play the doctor and treat your symptom (to whatever extent you feel comfortable).

4. Notice changes in how you feel physically and emotionally.
5. Based on this exercise, are there changes you could recommend to your physician or healer that would make their work more effective?

| PART TWO |

Flirting with Death

| CHAPTER 10 |

Stages of Life

Some specific transitions in life seem to bring us closer to our fears of dying. It is as if death is the sun, and we are planets revolving around it. At different stages of our lives, we come closer to or farther from death.

Childhood Fears

The first stage occurs in mid-childhood, when children separate from parents and enter school. This is a time when deep fears and nightmares often arise in children. Monsters may be living under the bed or in a closet. They may dream of being kidnapped, chased, or of someone hurting their parents or themselves. The child's anxiety level is often related to what the parents convey about their own fears around separation and life in general.

Parents convey their fears both directly and indirectly. One adult I was working with told me she had never in her life trusted men. As a child, she was told to watch out for men, because they can jump out of the bushes and grab you. This is a direct conveying of fear. Children also pick up on adults' subtle signals. They sense what it is like when they go out into the world with their parents. They notice how uptight the parents are when any separation moments occur. They sense the inner freedom of the parents to be themselves, and also to take space for themselves, including space away from the children. Children may not be able to verbalize this, but they reveal it in their dreams, their play, and through expressive techniques like working with sand tray or art therapy.

Our attitudes about whether the world is a safe or unsafe place come in large part from subtle gestures on the part of our parents. How a parent reacts when a child gets hurt or sick conveys a basic attitude towards the body. One attitude is to ignore and neglect it; another is aware but unafraid, while still another expresses panic and terror. For example, I remember a time when a neighbor child was over playing on a rope swing, and fell and hurt himself. I went and got the mom. She checked him out, was amazingly calm and reassuring, and then told him to keep playing. I asked her how she did this. She had twelve children. She said that after you have seen so much, you no longer act any more like a new parent. If it is nothing, you look, comfort, and send them on their way. This conveyed some basic trust in life, and her children were very courageous and independent. The child's survival at the beginning of their lives very much depends on staying acutely aware of and connected with, the adult. Through the connection, the child picks up many feeling-based attitudes towards many aspects of the world, that are hard to shake, even as adults. Thus the woman in the example above, whose mom told her to watch out for men who jump out of the bushes and grab her, has trouble trusting men, even men who seem wonderful to her. The child takes in and absorbs a great deal without digesting it. It is often a major task of adult years to find out what we have taken in, and then to digest it and make sense of it.

By school age, the child has also absorbed enough cultural norms that they begin to split off parts of themselves, particularly their aggressive, sexual, and playful natures. Split-off aspects often show up in dreams as powerful figures pursuing the child. Reassuring children and letting them know that scary dreams are normal is helpful at this stage.

Helping teach children that scary dreams can be fun to work with is also quite helpful. For example, my young daughter dreamed about a bear chasing her. When we role-played the dream, the bear turned into a dancing bear and they had a party together. Parents and children can have fun and do important therapeutic work through theater, puppetry, and other creative forms of expression with dreams.

Individual therapeutic work with an anxious child can be rapid and useful. Young children readily express their fears in play therapy, sand tray therapy, and art therapy. Some verbal children can just sit down and discuss what is bothering them. Individual therapy can help a child pick up and live whatever is terrifying them, so that it does not chase them through their dreams. One child I worked with dreamt of a big monster after him. The child had asthma. When we played monsters, he was a very powerful scary monster. He loved this, and this monster figure was actually very contactful. The more he got to know him, the less afraid he was, and the better his asthma was. Somehow the asthma was tied up with all this power inside himself that he couldn't let out, and just felt the victim of, through his asthma and his nightmares. According to process work theory, energy that is marginalized, like all of this contactful power, goes into our night dreams. What we don't live out expresses itself symbolically, so maybe he dreams of all that forbidden power as a monster. When he actually works with this power, it transforms into something not only powerful, but also very contactful and related. Working with him helped him to reconnect with this very essential part of himself. He discovered ways to play with this energy so it didn't have to manifest as a somatic symptom.

It may also be important to have family therapy sessions to discover what in the family system might be making a child anxious. In every family, certain parts are split off. Children, who are naturally sensitive, pick up and fear these parts. If a child is dreaming of something terrifying, it is most likely something the whole family has trouble living out consciously. If the whole family works together on their issues, the child isn't stuck with this difficulty alone. Another reason to include family work is that individual therapy may help the child integrate a part that was terrifying them. However, the family will still marginalize this part, and real progress will be difficult unless the family changes as well. Families tend to work on issues together.

At times, fears and anxieties may be sparked by past or present abuse. I remember one of my first cases, in which two young children were dreaming repeatedly about bears tearing into them. It turned out that their father was beating them, and the family was covering up the abuse. Until this fact came out, there was no possibility of healing the children's fears. When the state intervened and the children were safe, then therapy was effective in helping them with their nightmares. Nightmares that don't change sometimes continue because abuse is occurring; it is important for the therapist to find out what might be fueling such dreams.

Adolescent Fears

Another anxious transition time occurs when teens approach the end of high school. Teens often sense that something like death is occurring. Many teens have the feeling that attending school and living with their families is going to go on forever. Leaving high school is a shock that interrupts this sense of continuity in life. The life change that comes with the transition to adulthood is like a close encounter with death.

Often, teenagers translate this huge life change into physical problems or fears. For example, one teenager I know suddenly thought a pimple was cancer; generally, she was quite free of anxiety regarding her body. When I was in my late teens and going to doctors to find out what was wrong with my stomach, I was sure that if I could find and fix my digestive problems, then everything would be fine. I was in total denial about the scope of the journey I was about to undertake. Like most teens, I had no idea what it would mean to become myself independent of my family.

At this stage, talking with teens about how their identity is shifting, and how this is like a death, can be immensely helpful. In fact, quite a few teens actually become suicidal during this stage. For example, one young man I worked with felt suicidal and had fantasies that he would be appreciated more if he died. When I asked him what else might get him that recognition, he said that he hoped one day to be famous. As we discussed his excitement about his life dreams, his suicidal feelings stopped. Like many teens, he needed help with the transition into following his adult hopes and dreams and didn't know how to do this on his own.

Another frequent fear that teens have at this point in life is about relationships. When they have relationship problems, teens can become quite troubled and even feel suicidal. Many adults consider teenage relationships transitory and don't take them seriously. However, the importance that teens place on relationships is a message to adults that we give adolescent relationships and feelings their due weight.

If we take teen relationships seriously, we create an opportunity to talk to teens about the importance of relationship. We can also talk about balancing out the importance of relationship with other important things in life. These are lessons that will serve teens well in adulthood. However, many parents and teachers make the mistake of telling teenagers that they are too young to be serious about relationships. If we do this, we miss the fact that, for many teens, relationships are already matters of potential life and death, which the teen often needs help with.

It is very important that we as elders help guide teens through the initiation into adulthood. If we do so, their fear can transform into excitement about the future

Mid-Life and Death Issues

Another huge transitional phase is mid-life. I use the term mid-life not in reference to a specific age, but to a set of experiences. Traditionally, the mid-life crisis happens somewhere around the age of 50, but in my experience, people have mid-life crises anywhere between 30 and 80.

The anxieties that surface during late adolescence often return with incredible intensity in mid-life. There are many reasons for feeling close to death at mid-life. For some people, simply aging and getting closer to death makes it harder to ignore. Sometimes physical body changes, such as graying hair or hair loss, wake us up to our mortality.

Mid-life often means shifts in large parts of one's identity. Long-term partnerships often end or change at this time. If people have children, their identity as parents shifts as the children grow up and leave the nest. People may make career changes or be let go from a job. One's own parents often die when people are in their mid-life years, and the death of a parent shakes a person's sense of immortality. Health issues may become more evident at this time as well. Sometimes, all of these changes happen at once.

The mid-life transition can serve as an opportunity to let personal history die. In our early adult years, we often still identify as being from our family of origin, with problems based on coming from that particular family. Mid-life often calls on us to burn more of our personal wood around how we were raised and what kind of problems we have. We are increasingly challenged by our inner development to become freer and more whole.

At mid-life our dreams may be filled again with the mythical figures from our childhood nightmares, calling us to work on our long-term myths and development. Death erases our personal history; in fact, many people feel so free right before they die that they can clear up relationship problems and do other things they weren't free to do previously. The mid-life crisis gives us a chance to free ourselves without waiting for death, and also gives us a chance to enjoy our newfound freedom. Before the mid-life period, people may feel like victims of their lives. Mid-life provides a chance to shed this victim-hood and live freely, just as a snake sheds its skin to go into the next season. In some ways, it is easier to do this work before one is in the altered states and other difficulties of dying.

Jungian analyst Allan B. Chinen writes about this phenomenon in his book *In the Ever After*. Chinen believes that adults are more capable of dealing with early trauma in mid-life, when they are mature enough to recall and work through repressed memories. Chinen says that the detachment of maturity lets us step back enough to not get lost in these experiences. Chinen makes a clear argument in favor of dropping personal history at mid-life. He notes that, "Given the inevitability of personal losses with aging, this egocentrism is self-defeating. Self-transcendence is more than a virtue in the second half of life—it is a necessity."[85]

You may remember how Don Juan talked about death as an ally that gives us a wake-up jolt about what is important in life. The ally tends to show up strongly in mid-life, giving us time to wake up and live more fully. Chinen relates self- transcendence in later life to religious self-transcendence and cites the fairy-tale "An Old Mother's Sorrow" from the Brothers Grimm.[86] In this story, the mother mourns the death of her friend, her husband, and her children. She feels the terrible unfairness of this loss, but then begins to see all of it from the perspective of God. Through this larger view, she transcends her sorrow.

Chinen cites a fascinating study in which a positive correlation is found between adult interest in spirituality and psychological well being.[87] He points out that elders in fairy tales accept death as a natural part of life. In his words, "Fear of death subsides with maturity and there are suggestions that equanimity toward death correlates with mental health. Death simply becomes another fact of life to the mature individual."[88]

Senior Years

Late adulthood is another time of crisis when fears of dying often emerge. The central crisis around what a person contributes to society is a key issue at this age. This issue is becoming more and more critical in Western culture, which has a growing population of senior citizens combined with rampant ageism. Unlike traditional cultures, which valued elders highly, Western culture makes it very difficult to feel valued as an elder.

There are a number of issues specific to this period of life. At retirement, many people feel that they have lost value. While many chose to retire, many others who are still productive and creative are forced to retire, creating a true crisis of purpose. I have known several people who actually died shortly after a forced retirement. Helping people find what to do next can be an important part of therapy at this age. Often, people are interested in serving humanity as a whole. Creativity may need to come forward; this is a time when people may want to pursue writing, painting, photography, or music. It is important to deal with culturally defined views of the body at this age, as older people often feel that they are no longer attractive based on youthful models of beauty. Some people feel that they are not supposed to be sexual at this age, and feel in conflict about the sexual feelings that they have.

Health is also a big issue as people age, since Western culture teaches people to see their bodies as unhealthy and deteriorating. Some alternative physicians are beginning to challenge this idea. Chopra, for example, says, "Your body is aging beyond your control because it has been programmed to live out the rules of that collective conditioning. If there is anything natural and inevitable about the aging process, it cannot be known until the chains of our old beliefs are broken."[89]

Current research in process work is exploring the effects of processing deep issues on aging. This is a topic that Dr. Mindell has been focusing on in the last years, and he will be addressing this more in future books. My theory is that we die for many reasons, with biological reasons being only one source. Another source is that we get stuck on issues, go as far as we can, and give up. In his spring 2000 class on aging, Mindell theorized about the negative impact that long-term, unconscious hopelessness may have on the cellular level. If people are supported in working with their deepest personal and cultural issues, so they don't feel stuck for many years, this work might have a great affect on aging and the age of death. Chopra pointed out that so-called biological aging might be primarily based on cultural conditioning, and that as people clear this out, they may know what is truly biologically based and what is culturally based. In my experience, this is true. I have friends in their 80's who play tennis, work as therapists, write, are active with their families, and still work as social activists. If people were free to live out their lives free of programs around aging, we would see all kinds of older people—active, still, retired, working. If we open our eyes to this diversity, then we need to develop senior care facilities that reflect all levels of mental and physical well being.

Part of dying with equanimity is being treated with dignity at all ages, but especially as an elder. I am convinced that many people die before their time, or develop dementia, as a reaction to the meaninglessness of their lives at this phase. Our culture has an enormous amount of work to make aging a time of growing enlightenment and preparation for death. Unfortunately, older people are treated with such disrespect that many of them look forward to die. There are also new models; for example, the care centers where people and their interests are treated with respect, the physical surroundings are beautiful, and the food is healthy. We can only turn our backs on those who are aging if we deny that all of us will be elderly one day. I recommend that everyone spend some time in their younger years at nursing homes—it would guarantee that changes happen quickly in these places.

Arnold and Amy Mindell have proposed that feelings of aging may be related to not resolving issues in our lives; these unfinished issues may create a sense of mild chronic depression that people associate with feelings of aging.[90] It may be possible to restore some of what we identify as youthful energy by working on unresolved issues in our lives and freeing up the energy occupied by them. We may look at aging in part as the accumulation of tied up bundles of energy that, if untied, may provide us renewed access to the energy.

Summary

This chapter has looked at how we cope with fears of illness and death at pivotal times in life. In each period of our development we are faced with different tasks and issues, whether it is separating from parents, finding our path in mid-life, or aging with a sense of purpose. If we improve the sense of meaning in all phases of life, facing death with a sense of surrender and peace is a more real possibility. We may reach this goal through working on ourselves, and by creating a world that grows beyond ageism to develop respect for and humane treatment of older people.

EXERCISE

1. Think about the four major life phases discussed in this chapter: early childhood, late adolescence, mid-life, and the senior years. Make a note of which ones you have been through already and where you are now.

2. Looking back, remember if your fears of death or illness increased during these periods. Make a note of

which developmental tasks you were facing in each of those phases.

3. Ask yourself where you are in relation to these developmental tasks? For example, if your childhood task was separating from the mother, where are you now as far as separating from the mother?

4. Now try working on one of these stages and the developmental tasks you associate with it. Try processing the issues around the task through making up a story. Start with "Once upon a time there was this person with this and that childhood and this and that big task that revolved around this and that core issue." Next, bring in to your story where you are now with working on the core issues presented in the task. Then take the story and turn it either into a picture or a song or a dance.

5. Now imagine how the story could evolve into the future. If you are not now currently in your senior years, try and write down something about your most positive vision of your senior years. If you are in your senior years, you can still take the story into the future.

CHAPTER 11

Relationship Crises and Fears of Living and Dying

Painful relationship processes have the same potential power to wake us up as a physical brush with death does. It is also striking that people often experience the feelings that come up in painful relationship situations as if something is wrong physically. When breaking up with a partner, people may suddenly go for medical tests for mild chronic conditions or minor symptoms that they would usually not give a second thought to.

For example, after Jenny and Scott had been married twenty years, Jenny suddenly told Scott that she wanted a divorce. Scott went into complete shock, since he had thought the relationship would last forever. After the announcement, he began to think he had a major illness, and especially began to worry about his heart. He took the heart difficulties of the relationship literally, and despite his excellent health, became worried about his heart problems. If he had become as worried about the relationship as about his imagined physical symptoms, he may have had more of an opportunity to make changes. Many of us neglect or abuse our relationships and then are stunned when our partners leave.

Sally is another example. Just after her partner Jill left, Sally grew convinced that she had a sleep disorder, because she hadn't slept well since being alone. From the outside, it is easy to see that Sally's suffering may not have anything to do with her physical body. From the outside, it is also easy to think that these symptoms may be in part the physical effects of the stress and depression of the relationship crisis. From the midst of a relationship crisis, the person's only thought is often that they are ill.

The pain of a relationship ending can be as severe as the pain of a partner dying. In addition to working through the pain of losing a partner, when a relationship ends, a person often needs to see their ex-partner or may have to witness their coupling again with another partner.

Just as many of us do not expect our relationships to end, many of us also believe that our physical bodies will last forever and feel shocked when anything threatens that belief. For example, people often neglect their bodies. A common example is of the person who smokes for years, is warned by the doctor that they are developing lung problems, and nevertheless feels stunned when they receive a diagnosis of lung cancer. They were sure it would not be them.

Relationships and physical death share another commonality. Just as some people who have taken good care of themselves die at an early age, some relationships die simply because their time is up, their mission accomplished. Life is moving on.

Death as an Ally in Relationships

Death may work through relationships to shake people up in various ways. For example, even long-term relationship misery can't go on past a certain point because people start thinking about their death. If life went on forever, they might never make a relationship change, but people usually want to be happy and fulfilled while they are still alive. This pushes them to make changes in their relationships, and at times to move on.

Death also works as an ally in relationships because breaking up with someone you love, no matter what the circumstances, is a great lesson in impermanence. It is rare that people feel prepared for a break up. In hindsight, they may look back and see the clues, but often those clues were ignored until the end of the relationship. One of the reasons that people can miss the trouble in their relationships is that we have deep beliefs that relationships will go on forever; therefore, losing a relationship is an extreme lesson in letting go. There are times when nothing we do will bring our partners back. If we don't learn detachment, we go crazy. Relationship break-ups can be so painful that they sometimes do kill people, especially through suicide. If we survive the pain, we learn a lesson about the wisdom of impermanence. We learn that everything changes. Sometimes being more aware of these changes can help us avoid future suffering.

One way to be less afraid of death is to be more aware in relationship, to see the early signs of problems, so that we don't have to jump in at the end and try to give our relationships artificial respiration. Picking up relationship problems at an early stage has two main advantages. First, the person has more of an opportunity to do something, to work on themselves and the relationship, and to do this at a time of lesser stress. Many people only try to make changes under the gun of the relationship ending, and for some the stress of this is so debilitating that they can't do the necessary work to save the relationship. The second main reason is to help protect our systems from the stress of shock. Knowing what is coming may ease the blow, even if you can't avoid it. You can have your feet on the ground, and make steps in other areas. For example, knowing in advance at one point I was facing separation, I was able to start building the financial base to help this happen. Too often everything hits at once. Suddenly a person needs to find new housing, new friends, a new financial base, a good therapist, and so many other things all at the same time—it is like coming home and finding your suitcase packed and on the front porch. Knowing in advance can help a great deal, and hopefully this early knowledge will help all involved make an easier landing.

Another way relationship crises bring in death as an ally is in their ability to snap us out of being asleep while alive. Many of us are asleep in relation to our actions and how they affect our partners, and even more asleep about who are partners really are. It is as if we cast a spell on each other when we meet. This spell allows us to see only our highest hopes for the relationship. We miss all of the signals of where our needs and dreams don't fit with who our partner really is.[91] In a crisis, the spell starts to wear off. We suddenly see what we are longing for, and whom we are really with. This clarity may last only for moments, and is a contrast to the normal "asleep" state.

Sogyal Rinpoche says that something similar happens when people die—they get really free and experience reality as it is for a short time before they are drawn back into the drama of life and the wheel of fate.[92] Yet prolonged relationship crisis or relationship separation often truly tears down our walls of illusion.

For example, Frank and Peggy came in for counseling because Frank had never been interested in sex. Peggy really enjoys sex and is quite free in this area. Peggy is sure Frank will change if they experience therapy together, and thinks that he doesn't enjoy sex because he had a strict religious upbringing. However, no matter how hard they work or how much Frank changes, he is not able to become more interested in sex. After many months, Peggy comes to a startling realization during a session. She realizes that Frank is not sick; he just is not interested in sex. She begins to sob, and I ask her why she is crying. She says that this means she can't stand it anymore and needs to move on. If she stops seeing Frank as a sexually repressed person who might change at any moment, she suddenly doesn't want to keep trying to improve their sex life. This moment is both sad, and in a way liberating. At this point, Frank was completely shocked. Peggy was not who he thought she was; he saw that she might put her needs first. Peggy had seemed so loyal that he assumed she would put her sexual needs aside and stay with him forever.

The therapy climbed to a whole new level as Frank and Peggy began to let this new information sink in. They decided to separate temporarily to see if they really wanted to be with the person they now knew they were with. This kind of waking up from illusion is what the Tibetan Buddhists consider the central work of life and the best preparation for death.[93] This waking up occurs wherever delusions are cut through. One of the best places to do this is in relationship, where you can cut through to actually experience the real person you are with. For instance, in the Tibetan practice of Trekcho, "delusion is cut through, and the primordial purity and natural simplicity of the nature of mind is laid bare."[94]

Here is an example of how this works in relationship. Sandra had been with Paul in a seventeen-year marriage. He had beaten her several times to the point that she was hospitalized. As long as she remained the kind of wife he wanted, she was safe. Many years later she decided to leave him, and she was convinced he would not try to hurt her. She couldn't take the falseness of living with someone where she felt she was so ignored, now that she was no longer abused. One day, with the help of her therapy, she cut through all her illusions. She realized he was planning to hurt her. She probably saved her life by waking up to this fact. She had a few of her friends sneak her out of the house, and she went into hiding until she could move out and establish her own life and her own safety. It was not easy. She was so convinced that he had changed and would never hurt her again because he had promised her that he would not. It took all of her strength to see the escalating signs of violence and to get out.

The process of waking up sometimes happens in one big flash of awareness; more often, waking up occurs in a steady stream of discovering who you are, who your partner is, and what the relationship is truly about. In some instances, people can use these periods of increased awakening to heal deep old wounds.

For example, Jerry and Sandy came in for therapy when Sandy was ready to leave the relationship over Jerry's infidelity. After a long string of affairs and broken promises, Sandy said she was leaving. At this point Jerry became serious, for the first time in his life, about working on his history of being sexually abused. As he worked through this issue, he began to understand why he had affairs and was able to stop. Sandy's trust was understandably slow to return, but over time, she grew to trust Jerry again, as the infidelity truly did stop. In this case, the threat of the death of the relationship provided an opportunity to clean up relationship issues. The relationship went through something similar to a near-death experience and bounced back with the enlightenment that comes from a brush with death.

The possibility of the end of a relationship over one partner's addiction or behavior can go various ways. Sometimes a person can clean up the addiction, as in Jerry's case. In other cases, a person wants to change but cannot. Some people just walk away because the addiction is more important than the relationship at that point. Sometimes the threat of a relationship ending is the only thing strong enough to make someone serious about changing. In these cases, the threat of the relationship ending is like death as an ally, saying, "life is limited, so do what is necessary."

Eternity as a Solution

One solution to fears of death is belief in something eternal that goes on beyond physical death. A similar sense of the eternal can also help couples, who discover that when something ends, something else continues.

The terror I see in many couple's eyes as they plunge into unknown spaces in their relationship is much like the terror people feel when facing their own mortality. In both cases, there is a tendency to avoid looking at reality. I remember sitting with a couple when both people realized that the partner was not who they had thought they were. The possibility that this might mean they did not belong together was so terrifying that both of them started to sob.

Part of our terror of the unknown comes from living in a culture where security is so highly valued. There are few models for the excitement of plunging into the unknown. Facing the unknown, for most people, is like facing death.

We don't look at the unknown as exciting, but as something terrifying to be dreaded. One model for going into the unknown may come from spiritual traditions, in which death is seen not only as terrifying, but also as an awesome chance to see the radiance of the Divine. If we use this model for relationship change, we may see that going into the unknown in relationship might bring separation, but it might also bring liberation.

The death of a relationship can be an excellent time to work through primal issues related to one's family of origin. For example, when I was in my twenties, a woman I was involved with broke up with me suddenly. A few weeks later, she made a public announcement that she was going to marry someone else. I will never forget the pain I felt. At one point, when I was crying, I realized that I wanted to cry out for my mother, which was a strange feeling for an independent adult living thousands of miles from his real mother. I let out something similar to a primal scream, which felt like it released old childhood pain. Part of having one's personal history die involves letting go of the pain that our parents weren't there for us in all the ways we needed. In this woman's leaving me, I was able to go down into where that pain stemmed from, and as I released it at that very deep level, something healed in me. I was able to become more independent in my next relationship; I also was more conscious of my hurting, and what possible healing I needed in relationships. Healing deep hurts takes a long time, and the process still goes on, but that relationship hurt was a turning point in opening my awareness to clearing deep hurt.

This deep hurt is present to some degree in all of us, as no parent is perfect. All parents have their limits and make mistakes; in fact, part of why we grow is because our parents are not able to fulfill all of our needs. My own mother was a great and dedicated mother, yet there were unmet needs that I needed healed from as an adult. When I was able to go deep into the emptiness I felt inside, I received an enormous amount of healing from the break-up; the healing went much deeper than the relationship had.

The pain of a relationship ending often brings up past hurts, deprivations, and abuse issues. As these surface, the fear of dying can become intense, because personal history is trying to die. In addition, people often experience death anxieties when they feel abandoned. The child in us that could have died if we were physically abandoned at a young age often emerges at times of relationship loss. This gives us a chance to update our internal sense of self, and to notice that we are not actually children, but can use our adult powers for survival.

Behind our terror of loss and death, we may be able to contact special powers. For example, during a time of great loss in relationship, I had a terrifying dream about being marked by a huge grizzly bear. The power behind this frightening dream was my own grizzly bear nature, which I had to learn to live more consciously. This bear had to do with my own independence and strength not only to make it in the world, but also to fulfill my callings as a therapist, teacher, writer, and world worker. My experience is by no means unique; during times of great relationship upheaval and loss, many people dream about dead relatives, divine figures, or power animals coming to help them.

People also often have spiritual experiences during such times. Another example from my own life comes from when my wife and I were separating. We went on a trip together, as a sort of farewell. I was in so much pain, and everything seemed to amplify this. Even the fish bit me when I was snorkeling. Yet, at night, I had the most amazing dreams. Night after night, different spiritual teachers were there, teaching me, healing me, helping me through. It was as if these spiritual teachers were taking me into the next phase of life.

To enter the unknown in relationship takes a deep trust and belief that nature is behind relationship changes. The attitude that nature brings certain shifts in relationships is not common, but it can help us adjust to whatever comes. For example, separation is something that people usually resist, in part because separating can be incredibly painful. Surprisingly, when we enter a separation phase in relationship, we often discover that something eternal about the relationship goes on, that no matter what changes, a love that cannot be destroyed remains between people. This ongoing love is different from a codependent relationship, since unlike in codependent relationships, the harmful patterns stop.

This glimpse of the eternal may not only help people deal with their relationship loss, but also may relieve anxiety about physical death. Something ends, but something continues, perhaps to reappear later in life, in another lifetime, or just to continue as a feeling in one's heart or dreams. After I broke up with my first love, I had a dreaming relationship with her for almost twenty years, although I hadn't seen or talked to her for that entire period of time. In my day and night dreams, we talked and worked on our relationship. I came to grips with her being married and having children. On occasion we were more romantic. This dreaming relationship was both about my own feelings for her, which ran so deep that I still feel some of them thirty years later. They are also about my first love as a symbol for all my relationships with women. She also was an important dream symbol for a part of me. This particular woman was very shy at times, introverted, quietly wild, and tremendously nurturing. Over the years I have had to integrate all these aspects of her as parts of myself, and learn to treat myself as she treated me. Something died, but something lived on.

Some relationships seem to fulfill their unique central purpose, and at this point, the old relationship seems to die. For example, Paula and Robert had a highly contentious relationship. They were like two warriors constantly locked in a joust. Eventually, they both grew tired of this type of relating and separated for a while. When they got back together, the central focus of their relationship shifted to having a good time together. They went from being full of tension to bringing joy and happiness to themselves and those around them.

Some individuals and relationships go through many such cycles. After finishing one piece of personal history, they take off in an entire new direction, almost as if they go through many incarnations in one lifetime. For example, an intimate connection may die and be reborn as a friendship and then again as an intimate connection. A friendship may be reborn as a love connection. An enemy may become a close friend or vice versa. This type of fluidity is similar to what various Buddhist schools advocate developing as an attitude toward life and death. Rather than holding on to one state as fixed, we can learn to see a variety of fluid states of life and death. As Sogyal Rinpoche said about his masters, the borders between life and death had faded.[95]

In the earlier chapter on Zen, we heard the story of the Zen master who wouldn't say whether he was alive or dead; he was just in the midst of his process.[96] Many people have similar experiences at certain points in life. For example, when my marriage came apart, it came apart in its own unique way. We separated our living arrangements, but we still worked together, sometimes traveled together, and did certain family activities together. When people asked me if we were split up or together, if the relationship was alive or dead, I could not say either way. Just as the student got angry with the Zen master who wouldn't say if he was alive or dead, several friends got angry with me, saying that I should either be formally divorced or get back together with my wife.

Many people derive great security from having things defined clearly as yes or no, alive or dead, married or divorced. While I also like clear definitions, they don't always work well in relationship. Part of what made it easier to deal with the loss of my old marriage structure was simply to follow the flow of where nature wanted the relationship to go, into realms where the borders between married and divorced, life and death, faded away. My separation and the relationship after it were in some ways like a Zen temple where I learned about fluidity and impermanence. Some Zen masters carry a stick to give students a whack to awaken them. This marriage has given me many awakening whacks over the years. Many times I have gone back to dreaming that the old form has returned, only to receive a blow that tells me thinking that anything is permanent is an illusion. The relationship was never fixed, and I can't return to my illusions that it will settle into one fixed state. At one point, when we were having sex and living together again, I thought the marriage was fixed in stone. Over time, I came to know that, while I believe our deep feelings of love and connection are fixed in stone, the outer structure is sometimes like stone, and sometimes like dust in the wind. The most I can do is try to be aware of these changes as they occur. I can learn to be aware of the dream of the relationship, and the outer reality of what is actually happening on a daily basis.

There is a dreaming aspect to all relationships, which we are often not aware of. The dreaming parts of relationship contain the deepest longings and the shared development that we have together. Some people describe this dreaming, which brings us together, as chemistry. Others describe it as karma. Dreaming is the well from which our relationship springs; sometimes this well remains constant, but at other times it changes. For example, let's say that two people come together in their early twenties, with a central task of becoming more independent from their families. When they reach their thirties, their central task seems to be finding a worthy opponent in each other. They fight a great deal as they establish their individual power. At another point, the core of their relationship revolves around pursuing spiritual development together.

As people move through different aspects of dreaming, how the relationship looks in the world may also change. To continue with our example, in the stage when the people are leaving their families, they may cling to each other and spend a great deal of time together. While they are fighting in their thirties, they argue about many material things and eventually decide to live in separate houses. Later, when they are doing spiritual work together, they live together at an ashram. From the outside, by conventional definitions, this relationship at times looks totally together and at other times completely off track. However, if one is aware of the totality of the relationship, at both its core and its level of daily manifestation, the relationship appears to be evolving and meaningful in its many different forms.

Developing Detachment

In relationships where domestic violence is present, leaving one's partner can be physically as well as emotionally dangerous. While the loss of any relationship is a symbolic death, fearing death during some break ups may be realistic. If a partner takes a shot at us with a gun, it may become clear how dangerous they are, and such acts are usually a wake up call to get out of the relationship.

However, many times our partners take shots at us through their actions. While these actions may be just as psychologically dangerous as being shot at with a gun, it may be harder to perceive the impact of certain behaviors. For example, a person may discover that their partner has had an affair. The partner then continues with the affair, has other affairs, or leaves for someone else. Often times the one who was left comes to therapy reeling from the shock. Despite the obvious impact of the partner's behavior, it is unusual for a person to see their partner's behavior as detrimental to their well being. Often the person feels that if only they could change, their partner would return. I have seen many shocked looks when a person realizes that their partner is deeply hurtful and not just the nice person they always believed them to be.

For example, an affair that continues over time may make a partner become suicidal. The relationship pain becomes so great that the person would rather die than face it. In such circumstances, is easier on some level to think that if only you were better, your partner would love you more. Sometimes this is true, in that the affair is a desperate attempt to wake the partner up, and for the person having the affair to try to get their needs met. However, taking an affair as only about you can eventually become deadly. The other partner may be operating in a way that is not meant to hurt you, but does. They may be ready to move on before you are. They may also be operating in an unconscious way that hurts you simply because they can't do what they have to do and still keep you in their awareness. Sometimes people breaking out of old relationships are like bulls in china closets. They struggle so much to get out that they can't worry about what they break. Other times, affairs are meant to hurt. They are based on conscious or unconscious revenge. It is hard to see one's loved one as a possible source of any of this pain, and dying may seem more bearable than enduring what is happening.

The fear of death may be a reminder that the psychological pain involved in relationship issues can be deadly. I have often had to remind clients of this before they wake up and see whom they are with and what the partner is truly doing. Even when a person is being violently abused, they may still have trouble seeing their partner as anything but benevolent. I remember one woman who said her husband chased her around with a club, but since she hid under the bed and he couldn't hit her, she thought he really loved her and wouldn't hurt her. Another woman I worked with came in one day after her husband had shot at her with a gun while she was watching television. She asked me if she thought she was in danger, as the bullet missed her. Obviously I told both of these women they were in great danger, and we worked on steps for them to protect themselves. In these cases, their worries about death were accurate, because their partners were going to hurt them physically, and they needed to take that seriously. For most of us, it is not physical but psychological wounds, which may turn into physical symptoms, that our death anxieties wake us up to.

One key issue in hostile break-ups is developing sufficient detachment from the hurt caused by a partner that one can still feel the fullness of life. A critical task in these situations is for a person to remember that they have more facets than their connection to the partner. For example, Shelly had a career she loved, was a wonderful mother, and enjoyed her hobbies, friends, and volunteer work. However, when her husband left her for another woman, she became suicidal. The only thing that helped her rise out of suicidal depression was remembering that she was far more than a wife. She had a wonderful life and a real life calling, which she was ready to give up because of her husband's rejection. The ending of a relationship often feels like the end of life. The pain of loss is so strong that people often give up on everything else in their lives. It can be very helpful at these times to have someone remind you that your life is much bigger than a relationship.

In Western culture, coupled relationships are so highly valued that many people feel they are nothing without their partner. It is helpful to remember that a healthy relationship depends on each partner maintaining their own sense of space and personal identity as well as the coupled relationship. While merging identity with one's partner is ecstatic at given moments, if we merge to the point that we feel we are nothing without our partner, a separation can be life threatening. Fears of death in relationship can wake us up to the importance of identifying with and having a relationship with our whole selves, including the eternal part of us that no human can destroy, no matter how they may reject us.

Summary

This chapter pointed out how relationship crises, especially breaking up, can make someone feel like they are dying. We looked at relationship death, along with the eternal parts of relationships that don't die. We saw that people can learn about life and death processes through the parallel worlds of the body dying and something eternal continuing, and how relationships both die and have something eternal that endures.

Like near death experiences, which often wake us up to the reality of who we are and what our lives are about, relationship crises can serve as a wake up call. Many times people feel the same presence of death at the end of relationships as they do around physical symptoms. We can use both of these experiences to live more fully.

We also saw that there are real physical dangers, especially of suicide, at times of relationship crises. We ended by looking at the importance of detachment in surviving relationship loss. Detachment involves identifying with one's whole self rather than letting the loss of a part take over and create the sense that the whole person is finished. Like other crisis points in life, relationship crises can help us access our eternal self, which shows itself in our dreams and the mystical experiences that can occur around relationship loss.

EXERCISE

1. Remember a past relationship that ended painfully for you. If you think back to the end of this relationship, can you find anything that was right or meaningful about this ending?

2. Since that relationship ended, have you made some development that you might not have made if you were still with that person?

3. Imagine that you are the creator and destroyer of relationships. See if you can speak to your ordinary self about why you created that relationship and why you eventually needed it to end.

4. If you have current relationship, ask the forces of creation and destruction if they have an advice for you in your relationship. You may want to write down the information you get.

| CHAPTER 12 |

Near Death Experiences

One way to transcend the fear of death is to get a taste of it through a near death experience. Most of us have had mini near death experiences, such as when a car almost runs us off the road, or we almost suddenly slide off a cliff while hiking. There are also full blown near death experiences, such as when one's heart stops beating or one enters a coma. In this chapter, we will look at near death experiences and their relationship to the fear of death.

A Walk on the Other Side

Raymond Moody, Kenneth Ring, and others have done extensive research on near death experiences.[97] Their research concludes that between 35 to 40% of all people who come physically near to death, and are then revived, report similar experiences. This "classic" experience feels deeply spiritual, and people often describe it as an experience of love, acceptance, and peace. Within this framework, there are many variations. Some people experience meeting beings of light or relatives who have previously died. Some report being filled with knowledge. Many report being in cities of great light, or scenes of total, natural beauty. People tend to feel flooded with light and warmth. A sense of connection with a source of great illumination seems to be an essential part of this experience. These are clearly ecstatic experiences of most mystical realms.

In *Life After Life,* Raymond Moody describes some common steps people go through during near death experiences in which they were pronounced dead and returned to life. He bases the steps on common experiences described in his interviews with 150 people, although he clearly states that no two experiences are exactly alike. The first step is hearing the news that someone has pronounced them dead. During the early stages after this, many people describe pleasant and peaceful experiences. In the next step, people tend to hear noises, some unpleasant, some pleasant, and experience themselves as entering a dark space, like being pulled into a tunnel or cave. Many people then experience being out of their physical bodies and feel that the tunnel has taken them out of the body. People are sometimes disturbed by this transition, but Moody says that most describe themselves as having another body, a spiritual body. In the next stage, the individual reports meeting other people, some specific and known, others more vague, all there to guide the person through their experiences. The most powerful of these encounters is usually an encounter with a being of light. People report on this being of light through their own personal filters. Some say it was God, others an angel, or Jesus. The communication is not always verbal, but more of a direct communication of thoughts. Often the being asks key questions about the person's life. This often initiates the next stage, called the review. Moody says, "It is often obvious that the being can see the individual's whole life displayed and that he doesn't himself need information. His only intention is to provoke reflection."[98]

In some cases, Moody says people approach a phase where they experience a limit or border. The next step for all of these people was the coming back stage. Some came back through the original dark tunnel they went through on the way out of their bodies. A few remember coming back into their bodies. Once back, most go through a stage of wanting to talk about these experiences, as they were so profound. The next stage would be then to integrate and live out the changes that have happened.[99]

One of the most important points Moody makes is that people are no longer afraid of death after such experiences. He says, "In some form or another, almost every person has expressed to me the thought that he is no longer afraid of death. They all feel that they have tasks to do as long as they are physically alive and would agree with the words of a man who told me, 'I've got quite a lot of changing to do before I leave here.'"[100]

In his follow-up book *Reflections on Life After Life*, Raymond Moody touches on a further discovery that is key to the ideas we have been exploring in this book. He says that people in the process of dying, before they come back to life, have experiences in which they are given brief glimpses of all knowledge, including past present and future knowledge.[101]

This may be part of what leads writers like Moody and Ring to talk of the enormous transformation people go through when they come back. Generally, people come back from these experiences transformed. As Ring says

> The NDE (Near Death Experience) is essentially a spiritual experience that serves as a catalyst for spiritual awakening and development. Moreover, the spiritual development that unfolds following an NDE tends to take a particular form. Finally, as a by-product of

> this spiritual development, NDErs tend to manifest a variety of psychic abilities afterward that are an inherent part of their transformation.[102]

In other words, people return from these experiences more spiritually awakened and with increased awareness and psychic powers. Ring notes that people who have had these brushes with death place increased value on love and compassion. Focusing on love becomes the main task in life, and materialistic goals don't carry the same weight as they did before the experience.[103]

I have seen similar changes in people who return from near death experiences. People tend to return more committed to their spirituality, regardless of whether or not they had any previous commitment in this area. I have observed that people tend to value their relationships more, have an increased sense of life purpose, and care more about the world.

For example, you may remember the young man who came back from a coma and was not longer able to just party. He was clear about the kind of career he wanted and pursued that with unstoppable energy. Similarly, I remember a woman who was given only a 5% chance of surviving her coma. She awoke determined to live her life as fully as she had before. She went back to college and overcame the many obstacles of learning to walk, dealing with memory loss, and picking up her relationships as a completely changed person. It appears that people always return from near death experiences with a greater sense of connection to the spiritual and the eternal. If we believed that death was leading us toward an experience of the eternal, we might have less fear and a greater sense of peace around death.

Process Work with Near Death Experiences

While near death experiences bring people closer to an essential part of themselves, it often takes work to integrate the experience. One helpful way to work with a near death experience is to consciously pick up its message. For example, Kathy had been in a serious automobile accident. At one point in the accident, while waiting for emergency vehicles to arrive, she sensed that a spiritual force was present and that she would be fine. She became very calm and waited for help to come. However, in the blur of the aftermath of the accident, she had forgotten about her sense of a spiritual force. When we focused on the accident, Kathy re-experienced the sense of peace and divine presence, which was not part of her everyday life experience.

Focusing on a near death experience can be helpful in a number of different ways. First, people usually don't have easy access to the states that occur in near death experiences. Focusing on the experience can help a person feel more in touch with that state of being. Also, having contact with the spiritual part of ourselves is so important that we may have repeated extreme experiences in order to bring out this part of us. For example, some people are involved in a number of major accidents; if we assume that there is a meaning to this, it is easier to work on the experience than to keep having accidents. If we believe that there is a message in near death experiences, working on past ones might help prevent such experiences in the future.

For example, I remember a woman who had had repeated blows to the head and frequently got knocked out. When she went into that state consciously and role-played getting knocked out, she began to have visions. Behind these accidents was a visionary part of herself, which was trying to come through to consciousness. Another time I worked with someone who, by accident, drove her car off cliffs several times. Each time she walked away without a scratch. When we went into the accidents, what came out was how absolutely protected she felt. She felt like she had a guardian angel that brought the car down gently. Her goal after this work was to get closer to that guardian angel as a daily experience, and not just through potentially deadly auto accidents.

Experiences such as symptoms may carry the same processes that near death experiences bring to light. One way to work on a serious physical symptom is to explore near death experiences that the person may have had in the past. The near death experience can highlight the process that was trying to come to the surface in the present physical symptom. For example, I have never seen any young or middle-aged person with a severe cancer who has not had a near death experience. Working on these previous near death experiences can provide great insight into the present situation. For example, I remember one man who had had a near death experience at a time in life when he felt alienated from anything spiritual. Years before his cancer developed, this man was involved in a serious car accident. Although he didn't see himself as religious at the time, as he was waiting for the ambulance, he had an awesome sense of God's presence there with him. Twenty years later, in the midst of working on his cancer, this feeling of God's presence returned. He became a deeply spiritual man who overcame his resistance to organized religion and found his own spiritual path.

One way to look at near death experiences is as an extreme form of a message that we may have missed before. If we wish to live life fully, one way to do so is to pick up the messages that appear in our dreams and deep feelings before they need to appear in stronger forms. For example, the woman who drove her car off the cliff had dreamt that her car was flying, that she was in the clouds with angels, and that someone saved her while she was drowning. Working on the feelings and energy present in these dreams might have prevented her having the accidents in her car. Picking up the experience in the car before she gets hurt would be easier than a serious head injury that leaves her in a coma where she sees herself with the angels. If we can pick things up at their energetic states, they may not have to manifest in more serious and blatant forms to get our attention.

Summary

The growing body of research on near death experiences indicates that about 40% of people who have these experiences report similar ecstatic encounters with something deeply spiritual. These encounters often change their lives to make them more focused, and more interested in love and human connection.

From a process work standpoint, it is important to explore such strong experiences. If we can get in touch with the core growth involved in these experiences, it may prevent nature from needing to amplify them.

EXERCISE (best done with someone else)

1. Remember a time when you had a brush with death or a near death experience.
2. Recall the experience in as much detail as is comfortable.

3. Remember the most unknown, mysterious, mystical, or spiritual moment from this experience.
4. Go down into the essence of that experience and see if you can discover what you needed to experience or learn. Ask yourself what is at the root; what is the seed of this experience, which the bigger experience sprouted from? What is the most powerful, central, mystical, or numinous part of that experience?
5. Give voice to the learning through song, poetry, dance, storytelling, painting, or another art form.
6. Ask yourself how you would change your life now if you took this whole experience more seriously.

PART THREE

Becoming Eagle—Living and Dying Freely

| CHAPTER 13 |

Sexuality and Creative Expression

You might ask yourself what sexuality has to do with fears of living and dying. I bring in sexuality at this point because increased sexual freedom and enjoyment can indicate that a person is living more freely overall. The deeper one's freedom in life runs, the more fully one lives in all areas of life, including sexuality. The closer one gets to their own sense of living fully, the more passionate, fun, and spiritual one's sexuality becomes. Focusing on happiness and pleasure requires a shift in consciousness away from worrying, since it is hard to feel pleasure and worry at the same time.

Here is one example of how living more freely can have a positive impact on sexuality. Susan and Rod had both tolerated the lack of sexual excitement in their long-term relationship. Finally, Rod said that he was going to have an affair if they couldn't change their sex life. He blamed neither himself nor Susan for the lack of passion, but felt that he needed to experience his sexuality more fully than the relationship could provide. Susan agreed, and they came to therapy considering the possibility of a separation or an open marriage. During therapy, both Susan and Rod realized that they had come from family backgrounds that inhibited their sexuality. Susan's alcoholic family made any lack of control look terrifying. She grew up surrounded by drunken fights, which were often instigated by her father's affairs. Rod came from a religious family in which sex was a taboo topic. When I asked Rod what he thought about his parents' sexual relationship, he said that he and his sisters were probably born from the few times his parents made love.

Both Susan and Rod had entered their marriage afraid of sex and with little sexual experience. Rather than work directly on their sexual relationship, we worked on their family of origin issues around sex. Susan and Rod realized that they had both developed a fear of sex, but from opposite perspectives. Susan's fear was based on the family trouble around her father's affairs, and Rod's fear was based on his parents' repression of sexuality. Susan expressed her anger about her parents' drinking. She was angry at her father for his sexual lifestyle, and at her mother for fighting with him in front of her. She was angry with both parents for giving her such a negative view of relationship, altered states, and sex. Rod was angry with his parents for making sex forbidden. He talked about how his parents had quietly and indirectly given him a sense that sexuality was sick and to be avoided. He talked about how terrified he was when he first started masturbating and having other sexual experiences. In role-playing, he was able to tell his father how upset he was that he had not told him what he needed to know about sex, as many of his friends' fathers had.

Both Susan and Rod mentioned that their original families had avoided living out their deepest goals in life. Susan and Rod also had dreams for themselves and their family, but had been falling into a similar pattern of just shutting them out. They were also concerned that they were starting to drink to have a good time. With the help of therapy, many parts of their lives began to open up again. Susan went back to school, which was a long-term dream of hers. Rod started to play the guitar again. Gradually, their sexual relationship healed as well. They were headed towards a path of more ecstatic living, which was apparent in their increasing sense of purpose and freedom in all areas of life.

Creativity

In the previous example, Rod started to play the guitar again as he regained his connection to life. In cultures where spirituality plays a strong role, art and creativity often go hand in hand with personal power and spiritual strength. Once our life force starts to come back, it wants to express itself. Art of all forms is one way to let our life force live. More than rational discussion, art allows our deepest feelings and experiences to come forth. Other important outlets include social change and healing others.

In another example, Steve had been depressed most of his life. As he began to work on his depression, he began to play music again. The better he felt, the more music came out of him. Was the music a sign of his healing? Or was playing music healing him? I think that both were happening simultaneously; expressing our creativity can help us reconnect with the essential force of life, just as connecting with this force seems to call up our creativity.

Many of my clients have made major changes in both their physical body problems and emotional troubles by practicing writing, art, dancing, and other forms of creativity. Writing has been a central part of my own healing process. It has given me access to an introverted part of myself and has helped me find much of the peace I was missing. I often write about aspects of psychology and the world that I have been struggling with; in these instances, writing is part of the solution itself. Creative forms of expression allow for the deepest, most essential parts of ourselves to have an outlet, be it in voice, song, poetry, painting, or dance. When speaking won't get us down to the states underneath our symptoms, art often will.

Love and Sexuality

We have seen that near-death experiences tend to make people far more interested in feeling and expressing their love. Similarly, many people who are dying seem to transform; their fear of death often shifts and they become interested in expressing the love they feel. Love is a feeling that seems to transcend fears of death. We saw that love sometimes transcends the death of a relationship; similarly, love often transcends fear near the time of death. When my grandmother was close to death, she went through an amazing shift. Throughout her life, she was both very loving and very fearful. Near death, there was no fear left; all that remained was the love she felt for those around her. She faced death with the equanimity of a Zen master. I attribute her calm to the way she held love as a lifeboat to carry her between worlds.

People sometimes become confused as they know fewer bounds in their loving natures. As one client asked, "Does this mean I get intimately involved with everyone?" The answer turned out to be yes and no. It was "yes" in that her process seemed to be loving large numbers of people, but it was "no" in that they did not become her sexual or life partners. Sometimes, as love expands, it might mean loving intimately more than one person, but this wasn't her process. As people love more, without restrictions, they often notice that they suffer less around jealousy, insecurity, and other sources of relationship pain. They also start to love themselves more, which supports their relationships.

People who are really free in this loving "heart chakra" part of themselves have a sense of clarity around who they are. With such people, I feel relaxed and trusting. Being with someone who is free to love is like swimming in a beautiful clear lake—what you see is what you get, and you can see all the way to the bottom.

People who are free to love seem able to meet each person in a way that is clearly related to who that individual is. Their relationships with their partners, friends, children, coworkers, and other people in their life all seem to grow at once. They come from a place of inner abundance rather than scarcity. Their power source is infinite, so they don't have to worry about being used up or giving too much. They are as equally caring for themselves as for others, and therefore they move fluidly between taking care of others and themselves.

How does one reach such a state of loving abundance? Methods in this book, such as cleaning up personal history, having a deep personal connection, and being ruled by love rather than by fear, all contribute to this sense of open loving. The Buddhists talk about this kind of love as compassion for all beings.

As our personal freedom increases and our fears of death decrease, many aspects of life change. People often experience greater sexual enjoyment, increased creativity, additional love, more concern and energy for social action and world healing, and increasing spiritual powers. As our energy is freed up, we learn to fly higher and wider. Many people actually report nighttime dreams about flying freely as their personal freedom increases. I have seen this many times in my practice. One woman experienced her sexuality as a very painful area in her life. As an adult, she decided to live out her sexuality differently, and to only do what felt right for her. She was then able to create a sexual relationship that brought her much joy. She began to fly in her dreams, and even reported that one flying dream was so ecstatic she had an orgasm in the dream. She said that she had missed flying so much, since she had always flown in her childhood dreams—as freedom came back in one area, it appeared in other areas as well.

Sexual freedom has to do with approaching sex from the inside out. This means who you have sex with, how you have sex, how often, for what reasons, and with what intention. For example, Jan and Jim came into my office to work on their sexual relationship. Both felt they should be having more sex, and that there was something wrong with their relationship. However, after exploring this area in more depth, it turned out that they were both happy in their relationship and neither really missed having more sex. In fact, once they realized they didn't have a sexual problem, they felt freer and started having increased sex. Freedom for them meant freedom from the onslaught of modern media that makes it look like everyone is constantly having sex, implying that any couple that isn't having sex at least three times a week has a problem.

Freedom around sexuality takes many different forms. In another case, Bill and Jerry were two men in a long-term relationship. Jerry had wanted more sex, while Bill was not very interested in sexuality. While Bill had left behind enough of his family's views towards sex that he could freely be in a relationship with a man, he hadn't yet escaped their conservative, uptight views about sex. Their views oppressed him when he was in a heterosexual relationship years before, and still haunt him in his current relationship. For Bill and Jerry, freedom meant helping Bill free himself from his past upbringing so he could enjoy sex.

In another example, Sally and Fred had a great sex life at the beginning of their marriage. However, as the tensions built up over the years, their sex life "dried up," in their words. They fought a lot, and one result of all of the fighting was that neither one felt like making love, even though they remained very attracted to each other. They came in wanting freedom from their current arguments and past hurts. I asked them to explore in movement what would happen if they had no history. They began to dance and started to kiss. The work we did over the next few months helped them work through enough issues to rekindle their sexuality.

Finally, Leslie and Sherri were two women who had been in a relationship for several years. Both were successful professionals experiencing heavy work demands. They were both so busy that their sexuality and intimacy time dropped to almost nothing. They came to therapy looking for more control over their work lives so they could experience their passion together again, as all their passion was going into their work. I recommended they go away for a week together, to a romantic place, leaving their work at home. They had a wild passionate reconnection, and our work then became integrating times like this into their relationship.

Lastly, Harry and Jill came in confused about whether or not to stay together or separate. They loved each other, had a lot in common, fantasized about growing old together, and couldn't connect sexually. They also tried getting away on vacation, but nothing happened sexually. We tried puffing on the flames of passion in many ways, but their sex life only decreased. Liberation for this couple meant coming to grips with the fact that their sexual connection was over. They decided to separate. Currently they remain great friends and keep the door open for a possible rekindling of the flame between them. The main point here is that increasing sexual freedom may lead to all kinds of different results, ranging from keeping the same outer life and changing perspective, to greatly heating up the sexual connection, to breaking up.

Here are some exercises to help you explore your sexual life.

EXERCISE: Sexuality as a Gate to the Big You

This exercise is designed to experience with a sexual partner.

1. The next time you are making love with your partner, help each other notice where you stop yourselves in the following areas:
    - Movement
    - Touching
    - Making sounds
    - Visualizing or fantasizing
    - Feeling
    - Expressing passion
    - Having spiritual experiences
2. If you wish, try going a bit further and acting freer in any area. You may need a period of days, weeks, or months to experiment with acting freer in the various areas.
3. As the different channels of perception become more active, notice if you find more energy present in your lovemaking. This energy may spill into other aspects of your life, and the sense of freedom may help you

become freer in other areas of life, such as around health anxieties.

EXERCISE: Waking Up in Sexual relationship

The purpose of this exercise is to bring into awareness the signals connected to our sexual relationships. Working on these signals brings out personal and relationship issues so that we can work with them in tangible ways.

1. Ask your partner if you can reach out to touch their hand.
2. As you reach out to touch your partner's hand, both of you should notice all the double signals that come up in the approach and the hand touching. Double signals are any signals that don't go along with touching, such as looking away, hesitations, grabbing, or anything else. Go slowly and give these signals time to emerge and express themselves.
3. Amplify the double signals—take turns doing them more frequently until you find out exactly what you are doing. If you are hesitating or pushing or looking away, go into the experience and find out what that signal is trying to express. Next, help your partner react to what you are bringing in. Go into all the relationship material this brings up.
4. After discussing all of this, try bringing and touching the hands together again and notice what changes.
5. See if there are any connections between what just happened in the hand touching and what happens in your lovemaking. Discuss this together.
6. With all of your new awareness, see if your lovemaking changes. Go back whenever you need to and try the hand exercise again. Notice what has changed since the last time you did the exercise.

This final exercise is about using your hands to express love and healing.

EXERCISE: Healing Hands

1. The next time someone you care about is not feeling well, ask them for permission to put your hand on the area where they feel discomfort.
2. With your hand on that person, think about and feel how much you love them. Notice and feel what happens in your hands. Notice the person's feedback.
3. Now imagine you are a channel for all the love that is present in the universe. Try letting this love come into you, and then come into and through your hands.
4. Ask the person who received the loving how they feel now. Ask them to let you know if they notice any changes in the next day or so.

Summary

In this chapter we explored what different aspects of becoming freer in one's sexual relationship. This included looking at different views of what freedom might involve, physically, emotionally, and spiritually. Freedom involves being able to be yourself fully sexually as it is right for you and for your relationship. The chapter ended with practical exercises that let people go deeper in exploring their sexual freedom, and also what may be blocking this freedom.

| CHAPTER 14 |

Off the Wheel of Relationship

What does being free mean in the realm of relationship? When I bring it up with my clients who are couples, many respond first with fear. Their associations to being free are to an open relationship where you can sleep with another person. This is a very limited definition of relating freely. Being free in relationship may or may not change the rules of monogamy, as I am talking about a much more fundamental relational shift. Being free in relationship, or "relating off the wheel" refers to the ability to follow your own process in relating, including your own dreams, longings, perceptions, and intuitions. This means that the relationship is no longer unconsciously controlled by family or cultural patterns. It also means you are free to bring your whole self into the relationship.

Many long-term relationships have unexpressed agreements that limit how much of each person can come forward. One couple may say that I won't follow my career ambitions, and you put aside your creativity. I won't bring forward my angry side, and you don't bring forward your sad side. In Process-Oriented Psychology, these agreements are called double edges. These double edges come up in momentary interactions in couples, and can become long-term patterns. Let's look at Jean and Penny. These two women had been in relationship for several years. Penny loved to travel, and put this aside to be in relationship with Jean who had a more regular job and was not able to get away. Jean loved classical music concerts, but because Penny didn't like classical music, she stopped going. The relationship began to spiral downward when more and more parts of each person was not able to be lived out. By the time they came into therapy, they had almost no enjoyable contact with each other. Part of the therapy was based on unraveling how they had made these agreements not to be themselves fully anymore, and finding out the costs of these agreements. Emotionally, Penny used to get quite angry before she met Jean. Jean doesn't like anger, so Penny stopped being angry. However, Jean used to be able to express her sadness quite fluidly. Since Penny doesn't get angry, their interactions have stopped being very emotional, so Jean doesn't cry much anymore. The net cost of all this is that the passionate sides of the relationship faded. On the personal level, they both suffer from much more depression than when they met each other. Therapy involved looking at those choices, and also finding ways for each to bring in their emotions, which strengthened the relationship. One key session involved Penny realizing that it wasn't terrible if she got angry and Jean cried, but that it might actually be helpful at some points.

Another key issue is around how old family patterns still run our relationships. For example, let's say that I relate to my partner as my parent related to his partner, but I am not aware of this. Or I treat my female partner like I learned women should be treated by conveyors of culture, such as the media. My partner says, "Please change," but I can't because I am not aware of the fact that I am following unconscious programs. This concept is similar to how a computer operates. I recently had to call technical support because my computer kept stopping for a few minutes at a time, making it impossible to make changes or move forward on my work. Technical support informed me that other programs had been set up to run in the background. Although I wasn't aware of these programs running, they were stopping my ability to make further changes. The person who is free in relationship has done much work to learn about the programs that run them internally, including in relationships. Here is an example. I met Sam and Sally at a seminar, which they were attending to work on their relationship. Sam said Sally was always yelling at him. Sally said she yelled only because Sam was not present, and she felt furious. During the work, Sam had a memory of his mother hitting him. He is frozen in this place; it is the program he didn't know was running in the background. Sally's aggression took him back there. He then became frozen, Sally became more upset, and he froze even further. Sally wasn't aware of how much rage she put out. She explored what was inside her, and up came rage toward her absent father. In the world of programs, Sally is fighting her father, and Sam is escaping his mother. As both even momentarily become aware of these programs, they become aware of a parallel world in relationship, a world occupied by just the two of them. They see each other clearly, and discover important new information about how they are and are not compatible. If they become aware of the many different parallel worlds that exist outside the programmed world, they become free to make major changes and decisions in their relationship.

Relationship freedom also relates to having the choice to live either a more mainstream or a more alternative relationship style. My main practice is in Eugene, Oregon, which has a reputation of supporting alternative relationship styles. I grew up in a traditional suburb of St. Louis where I didn't know anyone who was divorced until I entered my teens, so Eugene has been quite an eye opener for me. Freedom around the form of the relationship means that people can create the structures that work for their inner psychology and their relationship needs. This may mean the most traditional, lifetime commitment to stay exclusively with each other, or may mean alternative forms of being together and being apart.

For example, John and Julie illustrate this point. They had been in a monogamous marriage for many years. Julie knew that John wasn't happy, yet he loved her and wanted to keep the family together for their love and for the sake of the children. Julie hadn't been much interested in being sexual with John for many years. She supported John in finding a lover who would help him in his happiness in that part of his life, and who could accept the limits and the reality that John was staying married. They created a relationship that seemed to meet everyone's needs. The woman John had an ongoing sexual relationship with was extremely busy and didn't need a full time relationship, and loved their time together. When they had gone to a couples' therapist, the therapist had insisted that John stop the other relationship, or that Julie leave him. This didn't work, and it almost destroyed their marriage. I was able to support them in finding what worked for them. Many of their problems stemmed from feeling badly about themselves for being non-traditional. John saw himself as a hurtful man taking advantage of a woman, and Julie saw herself as too soft, as her friends told her she should never let him get away with having another relationship. The more John and Julie worked on freeing themselves from this internal oppressor, the happier they became. Their arrangement took pressure off their relationship; in fact, it brought new life into it. Once they accepted their own non-traditional situation, the relationship strengthened and grew.

Larry and Linda were another long-term couple. When they first told me their arrangement, I couldn't quite believe they were being genuine, since I had never heard of such an arrangement, but it worked well for them. Larry and Sally had both been aware that the form of their relationship needed to change. They loved living together, enjoyed each other, and felt that all the romance, passion, and sexual parts of the relationship were over, at least for the time being. At this point, Linda met Fred and began a sexual relationship with him. When Fred eventually moved into their house, Larry and Fred became friends, while Linda and Larry kept up the parts of their relationship they loved, including their deep connection and friendship.

To become freer in our relationships, we need to learn about what restricts us, including our own psychology, our family history, and our culture. As we work on these and address the issues involved, we are then free to make choices that work well for us and suddenly the possibilities open up for the structure of our relationships. While looking at options of style and structure of relationship is often terrifying for couples, as they think it will destroy them, it more often than not helps breathe new life into dying relationships. Couples at some point can then make a decision to stay connected even though the relationship is dead or dying, leave the relationship, or stay and revitalize it. In my experience, couples that make conscious choices, in any of these directions, feel better about life than those who don't make their relationship decisions conscious.

Separation and Divorce

I wrote about separation and divorce extensively in *Vital Loving*. I offer a section from that book here.

"A process-oriented approach puts more emphasis on the feeling-level connection between couples. Thus, legally married couples may at times feel blissfully together, but at other times may need long periods of separation or intense conflict. Heterosexual, homosexual, and bisexual couples who are not legally married also experience a range of relationship needs. In this fluid perspective, couples define themselves from moment to moment. Some couples may often feel close, others may fight constantly, and both types may consider themselves coupled (or not). In this view, the power of definition lies with the individuals rather than with the state or church."[104]

Also, from the same manuscript, "What I have learned to drop is my program for what should happen in relationship and moments of major transition. This program-free realm is at times very scary and painful. There is nothing to hang on to but the moment. I find myself, and the couples I work with, in territory where there are few models, few guides besides one's own instincts. Yet the core of a relationship like this is a sense of incredible freedom that opens the relationship up to all kinds of creative forces and potentials. Death and rebirth become possible."[105]

And finally, from the same book, this next section gives my views on the spirit behind relationship transitions. "If we approach the relationship flexibly, the part that is no longer working may die, while the part with energy lives on. This couple might want to give up living together but keep their musical or physical relationship alive. In the old model, the entire relationship must end, except for certain legally prescribed forms such as parental rights. I think in many cases this is all or nothing approach is a terrible shame—we put so much energy and work into relationship that I would hope we could enjoy what still works well."

At a more esoteric level, these outer manifestations of an ongoing connection reflect the deeper dreaming process that continues after the formal death of a relationship. Relationships have an eternal side in that they are guided by myths reflected in the early dreams and dream-like experiences of the relationship. For example, I remember a couple who said that their earliest relationship memory was that they were out to dinner, and the man tried to do a magic trick where he pulled the table cloth out from under the dishes on the table. The magic only partially worked, and the dishes went all over the place and created a huge mess. These two main elements of magic and mess became two key elements that much of their relationship was organized around. The central difficulty of the couple was when there got to be too much mess and not enough magic, the woman would become disillusioned and they would have to bring in more magic. When things got too orderly and not exciting enough, the man became disillusioned. This relationship was not just about two people, but about two different energy states, magic and order, interacting.

I remember another couple who worked on the first dream that one partner had had about the other, in which the dreamer dreamt the partner was a drill sergeant. When working on this dream, the couple said that the whole question of authority and who was in charge was central to their relationship. They broke into laughter as they took turns playing the drill sergeant with each other. One of their central tasks was to integrate leadership, discipline and power into their relationship in a conscious way.

Myths are the central dreaming background to relationship. When certain myths are lived out, couples can move on from each other, or they may discover new myths to work on with each other. Some couples have myths that need to be worked on for their lifetimes. For example, a couple's first big experiences and major dreams might be about world change and social action.

This is a relationship myth one could spend lifetimes fulfilling. Having a myth that takes long-term work to fulfill brings up the eternal side of relationship connections. Eternal connections are not bound by convention, time, space, or marriage certificates.

Similarly, spiritual bonds are not made in the legal realm and can't be canceled in the legal realm either. I have seen many couples over the years who have done everything possible to destroy their connection, and the connection still lives on. This is not just co-dependency in which two people live off each other to form a whole. In contrast, deep spiritual connections are built on two beings who are individuals and also strongly connected. I have worked with many couples where a partner threatens, if you don't do this, or if you ever do that, I will never have anything to do with you again. Then the other partner has an affair, or makes a career change that the first partner prohibited. Despite all the threats to end the relationship, the forbidden act, when processed, may lead to an even more powerful connection. Relationships that are meant to continue in some form can withstand all kinds of relationship dynamite. This sort of endurance is not co-dependent, such as when an alcoholic and her partner support each other's denial. In a spiritually rooted connection the couple has to work through all that happens. They do not support each other's denial, but are instead intimately involved in helping each other wake up and become more aware.

Determining which parts of a relationship persist because of the spiritual power behind the guiding myth and which parts endure because of co-dependency is a difficult task. The best way to differentiate between these two possibilities is to observe the ongoing dreams of the people in the relationship. Co-dependency will show up as a repetitive problem in both people's dreaming. These kinds of dreams disturb one or both partners, irritating them into waking up. For example, in one of my relationships, whenever I slipped back into a co-dependent pattern, I would begin having relationship nightmares, which would stop only when I moved towards breaking the addictive pattern that failed to provide the happiness I wanted.

In contrast, some relationships are dedicated to helping people become free of their personal and shared addictions, and these are very powerful connections. If a relationship like this is interrupted on the daily physical plane, through separation, divorce, or death, it will continue in dreaming. I remember a time my wife and I were separated due to her traveling overseas. We had incredible moments of feeling our connection with each other, through the air, thousands of miles away, and somehow we always reached each other by phone at the time when one of us needed to talk. Even death doesn't stop an eternal connection. I have worked with adults who have lost a parent, and after the death have felt enormous shifts in the relationship with that parent. In therapy and in their dreams, they are finally cutting through old issues, and moving into increasingly loving feelings with their parents.

I remember one couple saying to me recently that their relationship did not have a honeymoon period. From the first moment together they were working on deep issues. Such relationships not only focus on interpersonal issues, but the issues constantly challenge both people to develop their whole selves. Such couples will often say, "Why am I with so and so when they push every button I have?" In fact, this button pushing can be a sign of two Zen students in relationship with each other, each supporting the other's enlightenment. Often from the outside these relationships appear to be filled with conflict and suffering, and external observers are often frightened by or disapproving of the intensity present. The relationship may go through many periods of death and renewal, and may need frequent help from a therapist. People who have this as their relationship myth seem to have little choice – they either work with their connection willingly or the relationship difficulties become so great they are forced to do the necessary personal growth and relationship work that is being asked of them.

Accepting Death and Change

Another side of recognizing the eternal aspect of relating involves accepting death and change. Buddhist teachers often say that the first lesson of Buddhism is the wisdom of impermanence. Everything changes, and our attachment to holding on to the way things are is a major cause of our suffering. Relationships are constant teachers of this principle. Couple after couple I have experienced, talk about how they suffer when their relationship changes, as they were sure that this relationship would last forever in its current form. People are angry at their partner, God, and everyone else when a relationship changes.

As a process worker, I see my job as helping people work with their attachment, pick up their detachment, and stay in touch with the eternal spiritual background of their relationships that will continue no matter how the form changes. Relationships that welcome death as part of the process also allow for rebirth. As the old parts of the process and old structures die, the potential for the new grows. A therapist who helps couples embrace moments of death in the connection opens the door for possible moments of rebirth. Therapists who try too hard to help couples hang on to the old forms and patterns may seem compassionate, but in helping the couple avoid death they maybe also limiting the potential for something new and exciting to regenerate the relationship."[106]

EXERCISE

This exercise gives us an opportunity to help us to apply some of these principles of free relating to a relationship, current or past, where issues of ending are or were up. The two main goals of this exercise are to give people an experience of following their own dreams around ending a relationship instead of just culturally patterned ways, and to give people a sense of the eternal connections present in the relationships that are facing, or have faced, ending. The experience of being connected with this eternal part often changes how people view and act around separation and divorce.

1. Recall a past or present relationship where you were separating or ending the relationship.
2. Imagine that you were free to make a more creative transition, free of the more mainstream conventional style of hot war or cold war. What kind of ending would you have made? Are there parts of the relationship you would have ended that you kept, or would have kept that you ended?
3. What elements of the relationship are eternal, and go on, even if the outer relationship is finished? Do you still dream about the person? What feelings do you think will continue for a lifetime?

4. What places do you think were addictive that you could have let go of sooner?
5. How was this relationship a type of replay of a family issue you grew up with? How did it help you resolve this issue?
6. Try writing a eulogy for the relationship, such as, "Here lies the old relationship with whomever. This relationship helped me finish up and process this part of my past history. Thank goodness that part is done. The part I take with me and appreciate is so and so."

Summary

Living freely in relationships means that people feel free to bring all the different parts of themselves to the table of the relationship, including parts that they themselves may need to learn more about, and learn to accept. This often involves learning to relate in ways that go beyond the ways our family of origin and culture pattern. Living free of these patterns unconsciously controlling our relationships is living off the wheel of relationship, meaning we don't need to just keep going around and around repeating the same old unsatisfying patterns.

Living off the wheel of relationship means being free to pick a form that is right for the relationship, however traditional or non-traditional as this may be. It also means that separation and divorce are a matter of following one's heart and the flow of relationship. The feeling states of marriage, separation, and divorce may or may not mean culturally sanctioned marriage and divorce. Together, separation and divorce become a more fluid, moment-to-moment, year-by-year experience, rather than just a legal definition.

Love also flows differently as liberation increases. It may be more love is present for more people. Sometimes people feel this love expand to all life. As this happens, it is possible that jealousy and insecurity may also lessen. People feel more at ease with letting their love emerge in their current relationships. There may also be less of a tendency to judge other people and their relationships and lifestyles.

Sexual freedom means being able to follow yourself as an individual and couple, without past personal, cultural, and family history dictating sexual or relationship life.

| CHAPTER 15 |

Social Change

Another sign of living fully is that a person has increasing amounts of energy. What once seemed overwhelming may seem easy to handle. A person's extra energy often flows into love, sexuality, and creativity. As their energy and awareness expand, many people find themselves increasingly interested in social action to make the world a better place. Social action takes many forms, including helping the elderly, developing environmental concerns, doing volunteer work, and taking political action on local, national, and international issues. Being connected to something bigger than oneself, and being able to follow your dreams of world change, have much to do with personal happiness and mental and physical health. The more connected we are to our lives as meaningful, the greater a sense of well being we experience.

For example, Stacey had a very difficult time struggling with various physical illnesses. She was lucky to survive one particular illness that almost killed her. When she emerged from this near-death experience, she decided to do something to make life easier for all the people who had this illness. Her world had expanded. In one of my classes, I asked people to imagine that they were free of all their past limitations and that they could do anything they wanted to change the world. I was touched to discover that each person had a hope to make the world a better place. These unlived dreams lock up much of our personal energy. Just being able to talk about such hopes creates a stimulating discussion. Each person had a major world problem they wished to dedicate themselves to; their goals included working to change racism, save the environment, further women's issues, prevent domestic violence, equalize economic disparity, and so on.

As people live more fully and freely, they often begin to live out their dreams. At one point in my life, my fears of death would never have allowed me to work in Israel, where I hope to help bring peace between the people who have been at war for many years. As my fear lessens, I have numerous, rich experiences that make life more worthwhile, and that make death seem less fearful. Freedom leads exponentially to more freedom. In terms of longevity, I sometimes think people die of boredom. For example, the transition from working to retirement can lead to depression, illness, and not infrequently, death. If people live their whole lives connected to social change, then this can become a focus for life when retirement comes. The Grey Panther organization models becoming world changers as we age, with their dedication to social change.

One of the most unexplored fears that arise in my practice is fear of the world. Part of this comes from what we project onto the world. We see the world as aggressive, competitive, and as all the aspects of ourselves we don't have enough access to. Another part of being afraid of the world has to do with traumas people have experienced in groups, including school and other settings where individuals may have been publicly humiliated, attacked, or abused. Because so little has been done still in the area of group process work and training, many groups still can be brutal on people. Groups gang up, scapegoat, ignore, marginalize, and act in other unconscious ways that hurt group members and themselves. This happens in all groups, including government, business, the medical field, and schools. Many non-profits I have been involved with do a great job promoting peace, or teaching alternative medicine or psychology, but can be just as unconscious as any other group when it comes to working with their own group process.

Freedom in this instance means three main changes occur. First, if I am free in the world, I have worked on my past traumas in groups and other world contexts so that I am open to experiencing something new. Second, I have enough connection with who I am that I carry with me the feeling that I have the power to help shape my world, and not just be the victim of it. This may mean having a clear sense of self, and may also include world work, conflict work, or other group process training, so that I am empowered to help shape the world I am part of. Third, it means I work on my own background and history, including my own cultural trauma also.

Much of our fear of groups and the world hides way back, outside our awareness. For example, how much fear of the world have I picked up as Jewish person who is still only the second generation of immigrants here to the United States? How much of the fear that runs through me is left over from times when, for a Jewish person, the world was indeed a very hostile place? Once I have worked on this in depth, I can see clearly where I am in real danger, and where I am traumatized by past memories and reactions that are passed through families. I also then can treat other marginalized groups differently, coming from a place of being in touch with how my history impacted me, and being able to understand from that place what they are going through. I also don't need them to live out for me the traumas and feelings I haven't yet addressed. The boundaries become clearer. I can separate my issues and their issues, and also know where we are the same, going through the same experiences even though the outer circumstances may greatly differ.

Another sign of being more open and liberated in the area of social change is adding on layers of perspective. This means that I am not just one-sided or polarized, but also able to see many sides, take many sides, and understand how all the sides are unfolding together. It may mean that I have worked through enough of my personal hurt and anger that I can be a true facilitator. For example, I used to get so angry when anti-Semitism came up in a group, that I just started yelling at the identified anti-Semite. While it continues to disturb me, when I hear anti-Semitic comments, I have worked enough with my anger that I can now spend sometime learning more about who it is that makes the comment, and how they got to be where they are in their relationship with Jews. In the long run, I have been able to bring about more social change by being able to have this dialogue than by coming unglued on people who make such comments.

Summary

Part of being free is having access to increasing amounts of energy, and increasing concerns for the growing circle that goes beyond my individual identity. As you work on your personal and collective issues of trauma, you can move beyond being afraid of changing the world to embracing your dreams of world change. Social action that comes from this place of your spiritual center has special effects on the world.

Being free to be a world changer means also being able to move beyond the paralysis of hopelessness. One person in touch with their personal power can make an enormous difference in a group, a city, or the bigger world. There are many women and men in history who created a more just world simply by taking a stand, and each of us has our own favorite heroes who have stood for justice, freedom, and our other highest ideals.

EXERCISE

1. Think of a world problem that concerns you, that grabs your attention, or that you make a real effort to avoid.
2. Imagine you had the power to really make a change in this area. What change would you work for?
3. Imagine you could make a difference around this problem. How would you feel?
4. What kinds of things stop you from working in this area?
5. Imagine that the obstacle stopping you is a person. What kind of a person would they be?
6. Imagine interacting with them or writing them a letter. Dialogue with them. Let them know why you want to change this aspect of the world, and how you will do it. See if you can move them out of your way.
7. Make a decision to take some steps to address this world problem. Set yourself a time limit, and write the steps down so you don't forget.

| CHAPTER 16 |

Following the Path of Heart Around Work and Career

Signs of Growing Freedom

One of the first signs of an emerging sense of freedom is simply that people start acknowledging the impact work has on their life. For many people to survive their careers, they must not notice the effect work has on other aspects of themselves. I have found this true for all kinds of work and for all levels of income, ranging from minimum wage to professional salaries. As people start to free themselves to be their whole selves, work is seen as a central part of their development and well being. People begin to be able to think more about being happy, fulfilled, and doing something meaningful. This is partially a matter of economic class and privilege, for it is much more difficult to think about feeling good when worrying about feeding your family. Yet, I have also seen people earning low incomes make decisions to leave jobs that are highly destructive to them, while some professionals making hundreds of thousands of dollars per year can't take this step. This is partially due to the hook of money. Money is a necessity, since we all need to eat and fulfill other basic needs such as shelter and clothing. Having money can be an important part of happiness. However, money can become a trap whose pursuit blocks out the importance of many other parts of our lives, including health, relationships, and spiritual practice, as well as our need to address social change.

Work as an Addiction

When work begins to marginalize other key parts of life so that damage is occurring, someone may be developing an addiction to work. Like most addictions, work can become a way to avoid other aspects of life and one's feelings. Many people overwork so that they feel they don't have to face their families or their own past hurts. For some, work is the only place to feel some sense of self-worth. I love working. It can be a beautiful and important way to spend time, which can not only take care of your own material needs, but also needs to create, serve others, be recognized, and be needed.

However, we must be aware when a line is crossed and work itself becomes the problem.

Work and Meaning

Our work life can be close to our deepest dreams, or far away from who we really are. I remember a woman in one of the first dream classes I taught. She said she had the most boring and meaningless job. However, she had amazing dreams. She dreamt over and over that she stood overlooking a valley, where an eagle came to her and brushed her with its feathers. I asked her what life would be like if she lived this part of her, the eagle woman, more. We tried to help build this more into her work life and daily life, but it was difficult. She came from a family and culture that didn't support women to dream big dreams, to fly after their highest aspirations.

For this woman, and for many of us, the challenge is to not only have these big dreams, but to live them out in daily life. Freedom to do this is partially a matter of economics and class issues. The richer you are, the easier it is in one respect to follow your dreams around work. However, I have seen multi-millionaires equally as unable to follow their path of heart around work as people earning minimum wage. I remember a time in my twenties when I was especially peaceful inside myself, and needed very little money. I had fewer money anxieties than my wealthy friends, even though I didn't often know how I would get enough money to pay for gas to drive to town to teach my dream classes. I also had more of an ability to do work that was meaningful. It was just something I felt and followed. When I finally had a great job offer, I kept the position until I felt that it wasn't right for me, and then moved on to start a private practice. Many family and friends were stunned, and warned that I might never get another job that good. However, I wasn't attached to it; I thought to myself that this job wasn't good for me anymore, except for my pocketbook. If I hadn't left it, I wouldn't be doing what I am doing today. Something inside me believed enough in following this flow and to be able to let go. As I have gotten older and have mortgages and a family and car payments, it is much harder to let go of work that isn't right for me. Yet, I still hold a deep belief that if I do what I love, it will also be the best for me, including financially. Thus far this has been true.

I try to share this spirit of trusting following myself around work and money with my clients. For example, Fred was a young man who hated his work. The only way he could get through the day was by using drugs. Besides the boredom of the work, Fred had a supervisor he couldn't stand. We started by working on many possibilities for changing the situation. We looked at trying to work it out with the supervisor, changing supervisors, and working on the supervisor as a part of himself that he projects outwardly and needs to clear up internally. Nothing worked, and he suffered tremendously. His drug use went up. Finally, I said that I thought the job was going to destroy him, and I was not sure it was worth it. He was young, motivated, and bright, so why not try something else? He answered that the outer reality was just too powerful. He needed the money and the benefits. He didn't believe he would ever do better. It was this sense of hopelessness that was exactly what he needed to learn more about. He identified where in his family history this hopelessness came from, in that his father experienced the same kind of suffering connected with his work. In fact, he had helped get his son this job. As we were working on this, a stroke of luck happened. The supervisor got transferred, and the new supervisor was easy for Fred to work with. He didn't have to go further with the outer changes, as he had done his inner work, and the universe cooperated with him to help him have a new supervisor.

In another example, Larry had worked at the same job for twenty-five years. He felt like a victim at work. People picked on him, skipped over him for promotions, and mistreated him. Larry was convinced that he would never find another opportunity if he tried to move on. Some of this is an outer reality. It is incredibly difficult to make it in this world without a good job. For most people, it is a struggle just to survive, and there is no time to think about being happy. Yet, this is not just a financial condition; it is also a spiritual condition. It involves not only financial resources, but also the deepest belief in the right to follow your heart, be happy, and have meaningful work.

Each person's process is different. For some, just working is enough, and they can't risk more to be happy. However, for many this is not the case, but they don't take risks because they are hopeless and about the possibility of a happier life. The level of risk is often up to the individual. Many people can't risk cutting loose from a job and drifting until they find their right place. They fear ending up in the street. However, many people just assume this is what risk taking means. I often talk to people about how risk taking means trying to create more options. It might mean going back to school and retraining, or starting a business, or something else in one's field. It might mean asking your boss for some of the changes you imagine. For example, Susan liked her job, but couldn't handle that it was full time plus. She never had time for the rest of her life and was burning out. I suggested she ask her boss if he were open to a job-sharing plan. We talked about possible advantages and disadvantages for her boss, herself and family, and the clients she served. It took some time and many talks to make the transition, but her boss agreed and Susan is far happier with her job now.

Sometimes getting free can be a matter of life and death. I have had clients who swore that the cancer or other disease like that came from their work environment, and here I don't mean the physical environment, but the feeling atmosphere.

One client told me that when she quit, her cancer treatments worked at a level no one expected them to work. When she went back into the field, her cancer came back almost immediately. In a situation like this, getting out may mean improved health.

Jill loved her work, but was always on overload. Her job pushed her so hard that she almost committed suicide from the pressure. Helping Jill get free was suicide prevention. Stacey worked in a situation where she was being sexually harassed, and her place of employment would not take her seriously. She was on the verge of a nervous breakdown. Helping her get out preserved her mental health. Joe loved his work, but it consumed him. He never had time for himself. In a relatively new job, he was making more money and had more stability than he had as an independent contractor, but he became increasingly depressed over his lack of spiritual life. He no longer had any time for meditation or contemplation. His inner life began to rebel, and he was willing to throw away his whole career if it meant being cut off from his inner life. He took the steps needed to integrate his inner life with his job, and began to take days off for retreat to focus on his inner life.

In all of these cases, people made steps toward freedom in their work lives. Those who feel free can integrate their jobs with their whole selves. They find work that is closest to their hearts, and often this supports their health, happiness, and creativity, as well as their spiritual well being. Oftentimes, at least in the long run, it also leads to a better financial situation. Sometimes people make more money from this place of well being, while other times they need less money because they feel happier. Rather than feeling like a slave to work, many people come to feel that their work is an intimate expression of their deepest natures.

| CHAPTER 17 |

Free to Die

Death with Equanimity

Much of this book has dealt with looking at how different traditions help us die freely. This chapter adds a few ideas not mentioned earlier. I have been thinking lately of friends and family members who died feeling terribly oppressed. One man was terrified of dying. The closer he got to death, and the more horrible health news he got, the more scared he became. He was overwhelmed with so much terror that he couldn't get any relief from his fear, even with medication. Only death brought him some peace. He didn't have anyone present to help him process all these different feelings about death. He didn't have the comfort of a spiritual life that offered a meaningful framework for life and death. I also think of colleagues who died long excruciating deaths, yet had a sense of ecstasy with their dying. They had people assisting them to process their dying. One gave a huge party and then died. The other went into something like a blissful state. Several of my clients also died in incredible peace, speaking about love as if they were already angels.

The central deciding factor in whether these people had devastating or meaningful deaths was whether or not they had midwives and midhusbands for the dying. This "midhelper" role might include hospice care, but goes beyond hospice to include support people who help those dying find meaning in their lives and in their deaths. All of us are both ordinary humans and mythical beings with huge dreams in the background. At death, these mythical parts are especially close to the surface, and with a little help, they come right through. It is access to this mythical part that carries us through our death. While it is possible to find this right before we die, I say, "Why wait?" It is easier to practice first and be familiar with these roads. It is also harder before death, because our ordinary consciousness has more to hold on to.

Here I think of one of the teenagers I helped in his psychological and spiritual transition from life to death. As his body was finally taken over by cancer, he became more and more interested in the dreams and spiritual themes. His message to his family became more and more clear. I will never forget his central teachings, which many of my clients repeat when they are near death. The first is to live every moment – all the good, and all the bad. The second is the power of love, and its ability to transcend life and death. The third is that God or the Goddess is not only a concept to think or read about, but something to remember and experience directly as a divine being, and to let flow through you to others. The word "love" has become over used. I sign most of my e-mails with love, and yet I know that that love is only a drop of what these people are talking about taking in before their death. I recently heard the Dalai Lama speak in Portland, Oregon. He talked about the importance and power of compassion and loving our fellow human beings. These clients of mine carried the same message at their death. I had the feeling that I was no longer the therapist or teacher, but was in the presence of a wise old master, whether the person was thirteen or forty or ninety. Because I had been so afraid of dying, I had previously avoided working with people who were dying. What a surprise when I felt myself actually more peaceful and feeling enlightened when working with the dying than with almost any other client population.

My current conclusion is that death is like flying on a jet. With a great pilot, it is smooth sailing and a smooth landing. With a person who doesn't know how to fly, nothing could be more frightening. Assuming this is true, it is time our work with the dying takes another major shift. Hospice care was the first main shift. It made people more comfortable, provided proper medication, and offered a chance to die at home. The next phase of development in our abilities to work with the dying needs to be that we train people to work with the altered states that surface around death, and help people to get to the mythical sides of themselves that can carry them to the other side. Dying has received terrible press. People who are dying feel so relieved when I tell them stories of other people's deaths that went well. They long to have access to all parts of themselves, which helps them move out of feeling like simply a victim of their illness.

Parallel Worlds

I can't end this chapter without mentioning a wonderful idea that has been running through my head for a long time. I often have wondered if we aren't somehow living and dying at the same time. For example, in our dreams we go to the land of the dead and visit relatives or friends who have died. People have other dreamlike experiences, such as having a friend get a message from a dead relative. Often such messages contain details the friend could not have known about. Is it not possible that when we are dead we are able on occasion to come back to this world?

In the winter of 2001, Arnold Mindell gave a lecture on parallel worlds. Drawing from his background in theoretical physics and Process-oriented Psychology, he gave examples of how we are in different worlds simultaneously, such as the daily waking world and the dream world. If you ask me if I am dreaming while I am talking to you, I would say, "No, I am awake," but if I go inside for a minute, I can access all kinds of images and other dreamlike experiences. My ears perked up when Mindell made a few brief comments about life and death as parallel worlds, which we may only feel as separate. Maybe time is only connected to one way of perceiving. If we could experience another part of our awareness, we could find that place where we are simultaneously in the world of life and the world of death. One more step might be to explore how we have access to all of these worlds at once. While I need many more years of meditation on this topic, I put these ideas out there just to stimulate reflection on this area of great mystery.

| CHAPTER 18 |

Living the Free Spiritual Life

This entire book is about developing spiritual freedom. Moving from anxiety to freedom is a spiritual journey. Working on fear and anxiety and moving past it is a holy endeavor. It consists not just of getting to the moment of freedom and enlightenment, but also of the process of getting there. There is no simple end point. The freer we are as individuals, the more people we can help to get off of the wheel of oppression. As we get freer, doing liberation work for all of us becomes the natural expression of whom we are. There are different signposts as people move along this path. As people liberate themselves, they often notice that their growth isn't so tied to suffering. They are learning more and more from the nourishment and ecstasy of life as well as from the pain. Another signpost is their growing interest and concern in helping more people drink from this river of light.

The Further Developing of Spiritual Powers

I consider love and caring for the planet spiritual powers. As people live more freely and bring out more of themselves, many other spiritual powers emerge. Some people report psychic gifts, such as being able to see the future more clearly or feeling that they can communicate over distances.

People commonly report increasing synchronicities. Many people report newfound abilities to recall dreams or to dream lucidly; that is, to know they are dreaming and to act more consciously in the dreaming state.

Other people report increasing healing powers for themselves and others. Once people start connecting with the larger spiritual part of themselves, they have increasing energy available for healing. I remember one woman who said that she suddenly felt incredible heat radiating from her hands, a totally unexpected result of all the personal work she had been doing. She was a massage therapist, and her clients began to have remarkable healing experiences as she lived more freely. Most of us use so little of our potential energy that we don't know what our healing powers may be. As we stop focusing on our own life and death and focus instead on living fully, these powers can come forward and express themselves.

Our spiritual path becomes learning and opening to more and more of these parts of ourselves, and then utilizing them to lighten the load of our fellow creatures on this earth.

This may also involve being part of an ongoing spiritual community, whether the kind we live our daily lives together, or the community that emerges when people come together to share key parts of our lives.

|CHAPTER 19|

Conclusion

Part of being free is knowing when to stop, and while I feel certain pressures to continue, the strongest voice in me says this is enough for now. Hopefully I will come back and address these issues in writing again and again as I learn more about living and dying.

Waking up to the process of dying in order to live freely, and living freely in order to die freely, has great implications for us, our relationships, our families, our places of work, and our art. This awakening also has political and social implications. If we wake up to living and dying, this awakening puts us in touch with our connection to all beings and to the earth. It is impossible to be on the path of opening one's heart and not to face the hatred and bigotry in oneself and one's world. Living fully means facing fully not only one's death, but the world as it is. Once we wake up, the unavoidable next step is to do something in one's limited life to make this world a better place for all people to live. Being awake and alive means being awake to the suffering of all people. The Buddhists talk about reaching enlightenment and choosing to come back for the sake of all beings.[107] Similarly, the Dalai Lama talks about trying to spread a sense of connection and caring for all beings on a daily basis.[108] This starts while we are here, now.

Shamanic cultures all have a sense of stewardship for the earth, a sense of needing to live close to nature and to care for it. As Audrey Shenandoah, Onondaga Clan Mother says, "I would urge the whole concept of nature to be rethought. Nature, the land must not mean money: it must designate life. Nature is the storehouse of potential life of future generations and is sacred."[109] Being close to life and death puts us close to nature, which changes our commitment to the ecological issues of the earth. Being aware of death, without denial, means being aware of how many species become extinct each day, how many are threatened, and how each of us can help to end suffering not only of humans, but also of all beings. Today, there are still enough eagles that many people can envision the soaring birds. I recently saw two of these magnificent birds in Eastern Oregon, sitting in a tree near where Chief Joseph, who spoke about the connected nature of all of life, is buried. Today, those eagles are alive—if we don't all wake up to living and dying consciously, and to our connections to all beings, they are likely to pass off the earth silently, as many species have done before them. Societies where people are afraid of death and life are apathetic societies. As we wake each other up, we will no longer tolerate the injustice around us.

I wrote this book for many reasons. One was the hope of lessening suffering; so many of us face anxieties about death and illness, and feel that fears restrict our freedom to live. My deepest hopes are that as people work consciously on issues of living and dying, as this book attempts to help people do, their lives and deaths will change. It is possible that both the length and the quality of people's lives can be improved by working on these core issues of life and death. It is also my experience that people who process their death beforehand report more positive dying experiences. All of this needs more research— the hardest part to research is if people feel in the after life, that having done this work in this life is helpful. However, people clearly are appreciative before death for having the opportunities to work on themselves to find the meaning in life, and the meaning in death.

Writing this book has been especially helpful for me. Studying these theories, and doing the exercises, has helped me to be more involved in my living and less afraid of my dying. I realize now more than ever that life is such a precious gift to be lived and celebrated.

I also wrote this book hoping to awaken all of us to the importance of building our world around love. Most people who have near death experiences also bring this message back to us. Death puts us closer to making this world a place of compassion.

Ancient spiritual paths offer us many clues about how to become the eagle and fly freely. Process work offers many different methods for working through one's personal history and connecting with our deepest selves. Yet, the choice to live fully belongs to each individual. Judaism recommends choosing life.[110] To me, this means that I need to choose living fully, each day. It also means that I need to be aware of death—not denying it, or obsessing over it, but simply staying awake to death's presence. I need to learn how the two are intimately connected.

Death reminds each of us of our mortality; from this sense of mortality comes a deep appreciation for the brief time that we have on this planet. The ecstasy, beautiful light, love, and meaning that people who have clinically died describe is actually here with us now.

Remember Master Bunan's advice?

Die while alive
And be thoroughly dead.
Then do what you will,
All is good.[111]
Bravely let go your hold
On the edge of the precipice
And die to the small self.
Then what is naturally revealed
Is the True-nature in which
There is neither life nor death.[112]

I wish us all good luck in moving past our dualistic thinking about life and death. When we are free of these, we have become the eagle, and can drink in the freedom of living and flying freely in life and death.

Suggested Readings

Bakan, David. (1991). *Sigmund Freud and the Jewish Mystical Tradition*, London: Free Association Books Limited.

Blofeld, John. (1978). *Taoism: The Road to Immortality*, Bolder: Shambhala.

Casteneda, Carlos. (1987). *The Power of Silence*, New York: Pocket Books.

Casteneda, Carlos. (1974). *The Teachings of Don Juan: A Yaqui Way of Knowledge*, New York: Pocket Books.

Casteneda, Carlos. (1981). *The Eagles Gift*, New York: Pocket Books.

Casteneda, Carlos. (1998). *The Active Side of Infinity*, New York: Harper Collins.

Casteneda, Carlos. (1993). *The Art of Dreaming*, New York: Harper Perennial.

Chinen, Allan B. (1993). *Beyond the Hero*. New York: Tarcher/Putnam.

Chinen, Allan B. (1989). *In the Ever After*. Wilmette, Illinois: Chiron Publications.

Dali Lama. (1996). *The Buddha Nature*, Woodside, Ca.: Bluestar Communications.

Erikson, Erik H. (1980). *Identity and the Life Cycle*, New York: W.W. Norton & Company.

Hahn, Thich Nhat. (1998). *The Heart of the Buddha's Teaching*, New York: Broadway Books.

Harner, Michael. (1980). *The Way of the Shaman*, San Francisco: Harper San Francisco.

Hau-Ching, Taoist Master Ni. (1979). The Taoist Inner *View of the Universe and the Immortal Realm,Los Angeles: The Shrine of the Eternal Breath of Tao.*

Hoffman, Edward. (1981). *The Way of Splendor, Jewish Mysticism and Modern Psychology*, Boulder: Shambala.

Sandra Ingerman. (1991). *Soul Retrieval*, San Francisco: Harper, San Francisco.

Kubler –Ross, Elisabeth. (1969). *On Death and Dying*, New York: Macmillan.

Kapleau, Phillip. (1989). *The Wheel of Life and Death,* New York: Doubleday.

Klien, Dennis. (1985). *The Jewish Origins of the Psychoanalytic Movement*, Chicago: University of Chicago Press.

Levine, Stephen (1982). *Who Dies?*, Garden City, New York: Anchor Books.

Mindell, Arnold. *Dreambody*, Boston: Sigo Press (1981); London: Routledge & Kegan Paul (1984); Portland, Oregon: Lao Tse Press (1998).

Mindell, Arnold. (1987). *The Dreambody in Relationships*. London: Routledge & Kegan Paul.

Mindell, Arnold. (1992). *The Leader as Martial Artist*. San Francisco: Harper.

Mindell, Arnold. (1989). *The Year 1*. London: Penguin Arkana.

Mindell, Arnold. (1985). *Rivers Way*. London: Routledge & Kegan Paul.

Mindell, Arnold. (1993). *The Shaman's Body*, San Francisco: Harper San Francisco.

Mindell, Arnold. (1995). *Sitting in the Fire*. Portland, Oregon: Lao Tse Press.

Mindell, Arnold. (1990). *Working on Yourself Alone*. London: Penguin Arkana.

Mindell, Arnold. (1985). *Working with the Dreaming Body.* London: Routledge & Kegan Paul.

Mindell, Arnold and Mindell, Amy. (1992). *Riding the Horse Backwards.* London: Penguin Arkana.

Ming-Dao, Deng. (1987). *Seven Bamboo Tablets,* San Francisco: Harper & Row.

Moody, Robert, *The Light Beyond.*

Moody, Raymond. (1976). *Life After Life,* Harrisburg, Pa: Stackpole Books.

Moody, Raymond. (1977). *Reflections on Life After Life,*Harrisburg, Pa: Stackpole Books.

Reimer, Jack. (1874). *Jewish Reflections on Death,* New York: Schocken Books.

Ring, Kenneth. (1985). *Heading Toward Omega, In Search of the Meaning of the Near-Death Experience,* New York: Quill William Morrow.

Simonton, Dr. Carl; Matthews, Stephanie; Creighton, James L. (1992). *Getting Well Again,* New York: Bantam Books.

Sogyal Rinpoche. (1992). *The Tibetan Book of Living and Dying,* San Francisco: Harper San Francisco.

Wall, Steve and Arden, Harvey. (1990). *Wisdomkeepers,* Hillsboro, Oregon: Beyond Words Publishing.

Weil, Dr. Andrew. (1995). *Spontaneous Healing,* New York: Alfred A. Knopf.

Winkler, Gershon. (1998). *Sacred Secrets: The Sanctity of Sex in Jewish Law and Lore,* Northvale, New Jersey: Jason Aronson Inc.

References

1 Sogyal Rinpoche, The Tibetan Book of Living and Dying, p.341.

2 For two sources of information on this, CQ Researcher, 02/25/2000, volume 10, issue 7, p.153, and RN magazine, May 2000, Volume 3, Issue 5, p.14.

3 Eugene Register Guard, Dec. 22, 1999, p.10A.

4 Mindell, Arnold, Dreambody, pp.10-11.

5 Ibid., p.11.

6 Reimer, Jack, Jewish Reflections on Death, p.31.

7 Ibid., p.68.

8 Much of my theory around health anxieties in families has its roots in the process-oriented family theory of psychological ghosts. A ghost is part of family life that organizes people's behavior and emotions, but it is not identified with or named. Typical ghosts include abuse, addictions, anger, fear, and grief. For example, in many families where an addict is present, everyone knows there is an addict, but he or she is never named as such and the addiction is not confronted. Denial reigns, even though the problem is right in front of everyone. Ghosts can also be happy experiences that aren't identified with, such as joy, freedom, love, or being childlike.

9 Gerson Winkler, Sacred Secrets, The Sanctity of Sex in Jewish Law and Lore, p.4.

10 Gershon Winkler, Sacred Secrets, p.6-7.

11 Andrew Furman, "No Trees Please We're Jewish," *Tikkun Magazine*, November/December 1999, pp.73-77.

12 Furman, p.74.

13 Gershon Winkler, *Sacred Secrets*, p.83.

14 In *The Way of Splendor: Jewish Mysticism and Modern Psychology*, Hoffman notes that "Inevitably, the Kabbalah tells us, our purpose on earth relates to our own precious lifetimes and those of others around us, especially intimates." p.201.

15 Hoffman, p.202.

16 Reimer, Jack, *Jewish Reflections on Death*, p.26.

17 Op.cit., p.30.

18 Mindell has referred to this eternal encompassing entity as "the big you," as opposed to "the little you," or ordinary human identity. Arnold and Amy Mindell have presented these ideas at a series of seminars, including the *Spiritual Feet, Buddhism and Process Psychology* Seminar in March, 1999.

19 For an excellent book on the subject of life, death, and Zen, see *The Wheel of Life and Death* by Philip Kapleau.

20 Kapleau, Phillip, *The Wheel of Life and Death*, p.XXV.

21 Op.Cit., p.XX.

22 Op.Cit., p.23.

23 Op.Cit., , p.27.

24 Op.Cit., p.29.

25 Kapleau, p.45.

26 Levine, Stephen, *Who Dies?*, p.5.

27 Op.Cit., Levine, p.9.

28 Op.Cit., Levine, p.14.

29 Op.Cit., Levine, p.179.

30 Op.Cit., Levine, p.15.

31 Sogyal Rinpoche, *The Tibetan Book of Living and Dying*, p.12.

32 This particular work is highly accessible to Westerners, who may have had less exposure to Buddhist philosophy.

33 Sogyal Rinpoche, *The Tibetan Book of Living and Dying*, p.8.

34 Op.Cit., p.40.

35 Sogyal Rinpoche, *The Tibetan Book of Living and Dying*, p.14.

36 Op. Cit., p.108.

37 Op.Cit., p.236.

38 Sogyal Rinpoche, p.231-235.

39 Sogyal Rinpoche, p.303.

40 Readers may be interested in reading any of Casteneda's books, or Michael Harner's *The Way of the Shaman*, for more detailed information about shamanism.

41 Casteneda, Carlos, *The Power of Silence*, p.109.

42 The term sorcerer refers to a person who has developed their awareness to a greater extent than the average human.

43 Op.Cit., pp.109-110.

44 Op.Cit., p.112.

45 Ibid.

46 Casteneda, *The Power of Silence*, p.195.

47 Casteneda, Carlos, *The Active Side of Infinity*, p.148.

48 Ibid.

49 Mindell, Arnold, the Shamans Body, p.157.

50 Ibid.

51 Casteneda, Carlos, The Power of Silence, p.17.

52 These areas have also all been utilized by artists in every era.

53 See any of Raymond Moody's books for more on this topic.

54 This is a form of shape-shifting, a shamanic technique in which the shaman takes on other forms.

55 I include Process Work as a spiritual approach, since it focuses on the level of the Big You.

56 Blofeld, John. *Taoism: The Road to Immortality*, p.24.

57 I draw this conclusion from having spent so many hours with coma patients of all ages, nationalities, with many different sources of coma including head injury, asthma attack, stroke, heart attack, brain tumors, and drowning. More on the theory and practice of coma work can be found in *Coma; Key to Awakening*, by Arnold Mindell, and *Coma; a Healing Journey*, by Amy Mindell.

58 Blofeld, John, *Taoism, The Road to Immortality*, p.10.

59 Blofeld, p.10.

60 Ibid.

61 Blofeld, p.14.

62 Blofeld, p.15.

63 Taoist Master Ni Hau-Ching, *The Taoist Inner View of the Universe and the Immortal Realm*, p.70.

64 Master Ni Hau-Ching, p.71.

65 In Blofeld, John, *Taoism, The Road to Immortality*, p.50.

66 Ni Hau-Ching, *The Taoist Inner View of the Universe and the Immortal Realm*, p.72.

67 Blofeld, John, p.16.

68 The entire list can be found in Ni Hau Ching, The Taoist Inner View of the Universe and the Immortal Realm, pp.115-117.

69 Sandra Ingerman, Soul Retrieval, p.11-12.

70 Ingerman, p.17.

71 An excellent source on this kind of ritual work in shamanism is Sandra Ingerman, *Soul Retrieval*, pp.32-33. Also helpful is Michael Harner's *Way of the Shaman*.

72 Dr. Jack Weissman, infectious disease specialist, in Kapleau, Phillip, *The Wheel of Life and Death*, p.8.

73 Reimer, Jack, *Jewish Reflections on Death*, p.7.

74 Register Guard, June 11.2000, p.5A.

75 Weil, Andrew, *Spontaneous Healing*, p.64.

76 Weil, Andrew, *Spontaneous Healing*, p.64.

77 People interested in Simonton's work might look at his book *Getting Well Again*, written with Stephanie Matthews and James L. Creighton, Bantam Books, New York, 1992.

78 Weil, Andrew, *Spontaneous Healing*, p.59.

79 Weil, Andrew, *Spontaneous Healing*, p.63.

80 Op.Cit., p.60.

81 Weil, Andrew, *Spontaneous Healing*, pp.225-226.

82 Register Guard, July10,2000, p.4D.

83 Oregon Health Sciences Institute in Portland, Oregon, also integrates art.

84 Weil, Andrew, *Spontaneous Healing*, p.6.

85 Chinen, Allan B., *In the Ever After*, p.52.

86 Chinen, Allan, *In the Ever After*, pp.57-64, from "The Aged Mother," in J Grimm, The Complete Grimm's Fairy Tales.

87 Chinen, p.52.

88 Chinen, p.64.

89 Chopra, Deepak, *Ageless Body Timeless Mind*, p.3.

90 Arnold and Amy Mindell, *Quantum Medicine Seminar*, Spring 2000.

91 Sogyal Rinpoche, *The Tibetan Book of Living and Dying*, p.282.

92 Ibid.

93 Sogyal Rinpoche, *The Tibetan Book of Living and Dying*, p.167.

94 Sogyal Rinpoche, *The Tibetan Book of Living and Dying*, p.183.

95 Kapleau, Philip, *The Wheel of Life and Death*, p.123.

96 Ring, Kenneth, Heading Toward Omega, p.35.

97 Moody, Raymond, *Life After Life*, p.49.

98 Moody, Raymond, *Life After Life*, pp.23-67.

99 Moody, Raymond, *Life After Life*, p.68.

100 Moody, Raymond, *Reflections on Life After Life*, p.18.

101 Ring, Kenneth, *Heading Towards Omega: in Search of the Meaning of the Near Death Experience*, p.51.

102 Ring, Kenneth, *Heading Toward Omega*, p.141.

103 Gary Reiss, Transform Your Family, unpublished manuscript p.27.

104 Op.cit., p.34.

105 Op. Cit., p.34-39.

106 Thich Nhat Hanh, *The Heart of the Buddha's Teaching*, p.245.

107 The Dalai Lama, *The Buddha Nature*, p.78.

108 Steve Wall and Harvey Arden, *Wisdom Keepers*, p.27.

109 Reimer, Jack, *Jewish Reflections on Death*, p.68.

110 Kapleau, Philip, *The Wheel of Life and Death*, p.46.

111 Kapleau, p.45.

Index

C

D

G

H

I

J

K

L

M

U

V

W

Z